THE REIVERS WAY

About the Author

Paddy Dillon is a prolific walker and guidebook writer, with over 40 books to his name and contributions to 25 other books. He has written extensively for several outdoor magazines and other publications and has appeared on radio and television.

Paddy has walked extensively around all parts of Northumberland over many decades, in all weathers and seasons. In this guidebook he explores the long-distance Reivers Way, which links many of the county's classic walking areas. Paddy uses a palmtop computer to write his route descriptions while walking, taking note of useful facilities along the way. His descriptions are therefore precise, having been written at the very point at which the reader uses them.

Paddy is an indefatigable long-distance walker who has walked all of Britain's National Trails and several major European trails. He lives on the fringes of the English Lake District and has walked, and written about walking, in every county throughout the British Isles. He has led guided walking holidays and has walked throughout Europe, as well as Nepal, Tibet, and the Rocky Mountains of Canada and the US. Paddy is a member of the Outdoor Writers and Photographers Guild.

Other Cicerone guides by Paddy Dillon

THE REIVERS WAY

by Paddy Dillon

2 POLICE SQUARE, MILNTHORPE, CUMBRIA LA7 7PY
www.cicerone.co.uk

© Paddy Dillon 2009
First edition 2009
ISBN-13: 978 1 85284 498 1

A catalogue record for this book is available from the British Library.

Advice to Readers

Readers are advised that, while every effort is made by our authors to
ensure the accuracy of guidebooks as they go to print, changes can occur
during the lifetime of an edition. Please check the Cicerone website (www.
cicerone.co.uk) for any updates before planning your trip. It is also advisable
to check information on such things as transport, accommodation and shops
locally. Even rights of way can be altered over time. We are always grateful
for information about any discrepancies between a guidebook and the facts
on the ground, sent by email to info@cicerone.co.uk or by post to 2, Police
Square, Milnthorpe LA7 7PY.

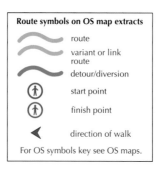

Front cover: Walking in the summer months means long daylight hours and
generally good weather on the high moors.

CONTENTS

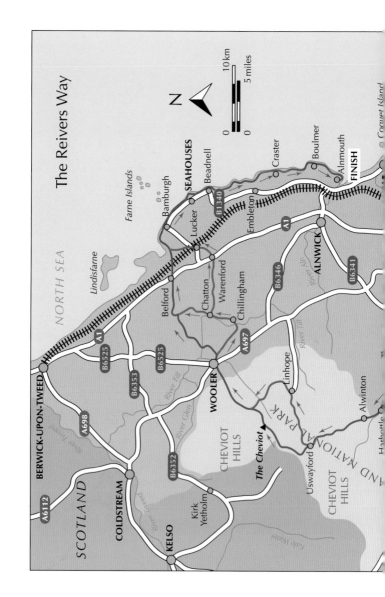

The Reivers Way

The solitary farmhouse at Uswayford provides lodgings and meals in the very heart of the Cheviot Hills

PREFACE

Large herds of dairy and beef cattle are reared in the broad and sprawling Northumberland countryside

I never met the late James Roberts, author of Cicerone's original guide to the Reivers Way, but if I had I'm sure I would have recognised a kindred spirit. Roberts' enthusiasm for Northumberland spanned many years, and his guidebook to the Reivers Way was penned while walking the route on his honeymoon in September 1992. Ten years earlier he had acquired a simple, stapled booklet covering the route, written by Harold Osmond Wade, itself dating from 1977. This small guide was pieced together from articles written by Wade for the *Newcastle Chronicle,* in which he serialised a trip he made piecemeal around the Reivers Way during the summer of 1975.

Wade was an authority on the Northumberland countryside, but he wouldn't have written about the Reivers Way without being inspired by Ken Coulson. As for Coulson, he entered a competition called 'To the Hills', run by Radio Newcastle, winning it with his idea for the route we now know as the Reivers Way. The Reivers Way is therefore essentially a creation of the 1970s.

While writing my own guidebook to the route for Cicerone, reflecting the designation of large areas of 'access land' in 2000 among other changes over the past 10 years, I have enjoyed revisiting many of my own favourite parts of Northumberland, walking the Reivers Way in summer and winter. I hope walkers will, as I do, remember as they follow the route Coulson, Wade and Roberts, who first encouraged others to explore and appreciate the wild countryside and fascinating heritage of Northumberland.

Paddy Dillon

Food, drink, accommodation and other facilities are available in towns and villages along the Reivers Way

INTRODUCTION

The Reivers Way is an 'unofficial' long-distance trail, wandering some 240km (150 miles) round the sparsely populated border county of Northumberland. While the popular Pennine Way and Hadrian's Wall national trails run across Northumberland, the Reivers Way almost encircles the county, offering a wonderful opportunity to explore its wildest and most scenic parts. The route can be walked in nine days, and is suitable for an average walker, provided that they are reasonably competent with a map and compass. The route is not specifically waymarked beyond the usual public footpath and bridleway signposts, but the local authority has declared its intention to ensure that the paths are maintained in good order.

The trail starts at Corbridge and crosses Hexamshire Common in the North Pennines Area of Outstanding Natural Beauty. After following part of Hadrian's Wall, a series of fine little towns and villages are visited, including Wark, Elsdon and Rothbury, as the route heads in and out of the Northumberland National Park. The broad and bleak Cheviot Hills are crossed on the way to Wooler. After catching a glimpse of Lindisfarne, the route traces the scenic Northumberland Heritage Coast from Bamburgh to Seahouses, then onwards to Craster and Boulmer to finish at Alnmouth. With an extra day to hand, walkers can include a boat trip to the bird reserves on the Farne Islands.

The Reivers Way is not based on any particular route used by reivers and 'moss troopers', but is simply a celebration of their memory, and a fine way to explore the land where they lived, and often died, in violent circumstances. When stripped of romance and glamour, reivers were little more than robbers and cattle rustlers living in a largely lawless society, but most of them had no option but to rob and raid in order to feed themselves and their families.

BRIEF HISTORY OF A BORDERLAND

Northumberland was forever destined to be 'border country' because of its position at the narrowest point of Great Britain. Evidence of human activity dates back 6000 years, and the region is well endowed with ancient settlement sites and ritual monuments. The Bronze Age and Iron Age were characterised by a noticeable level of strife, with many settlements built on defensive sites. A Celtic tribe, the Votadini, pushed southwards from Scotland, and was no doubt culturally distinct from other tribes already occupying the region.

The Romans reinforced any existing cultural divide when they constructed Hadrian's Wall in 122AD

Roman legions marched northwards through Britain between 55BC and 77AD, confidently claiming a complete conquest. However, while southern Britain was gradually Romanised, northern Britain rebelled. Any existing cultural border was well and truly reinforced with the building of Hadrian's Wall from coast to coast in 122AD. There was another push northwards, resulting in the construction of the Antonine Wall in 142AD, but the legions had to pull back to Hadrian's Wall in 160AD. It seems the Romans paid the Celtic Votadini to keep the Picts at bay to the north.

Under pressure from many sides, the Romans withdrew from Britain in 410AD. While Hadrian's Wall is now in ruins, there is still a tangible feeling of being in 'border country' while

following it. The Celts and Picts suffered as much from internecine strife as they did from fighting each other, and they were both overrun by Angles and Saxons.

Ida 'the Flamebearer' was an Angle who established a base at Bamburgh in 547AD. From this long-fortified rocky eminence he began to carve the foundations of a kingdom that became known as Northumbria, spreading far beyond current-day Northumberland. Successive Anglo-Saxon Northumbrian kings established a reasonable level of peace, while King Oswald encouraged Celtic Christian communities to flourish, spreading onto the mainland from Lindisfarne. Notable among the early churchmen were Aidan and Cuthbert. Danish invaders made incursions into the region, starting with an attack on Lindisfarne in 793AD. Later, the Scots also raided the region.

After the Norman Conquest another period of relative peace endured from the 11th to 13th centuries, with the Earls of Northumberland administering the region. Large-scale construction projects included castles and monasteries, especially along the coast and on the fertile lowlands. The death of Alexander III of Scotland in 1285, and the rise of Edward II of England, sowed the seeds of centuries of border strife. The local population found themselves under attack from all sides, with few they could truly call friends.

There was no convenient 'border' between England and Scotland drawn on the map, just a region of wild country that neither side could claim as their own, or hold against the other. Armies marched back and forth, demanding or appropriating provisions, so that the local population found itself reduced to poverty and starvation. They responded as desperate people always do, by going out and taking whatever they needed, from wherever they could find it.

The Borders were essentially lawless, but certain codes of conduct were observed, and the most enduring allegiances of all were bonds of blood between close family members. About one hundred surnames are recognised as 'reiver' family names, spanning the alphabet from Ainslie to Young.

Despite England and Scotland being locked in a state of permanent warfare for over three centuries, both

The decayed drum towers flanking the entrance to Dunstanburgh Castle on the Northumberland coast (Day 9)

Reivers rustled cattle in the remote and sparsely populated borderlands between England and Scotland

nations had to tackle border lawlessness, so the region was divided into three 'marches'. In Northumberland the problem was not simply English versus Scots across a fluid border, but reivers from Tynedale and Redesdale frequently raiding the fertile plains of Northumberland. Each march had two wardens – one English and one Scottish – to oversee rudimentary law and order. Scottish wardens were generally appointed from the local gentry, so had a good understanding of local issues, but were prone to corruption. English wardens were generally appointed from outside the area, so were less prone to corruption, but more inclined to misunderstand situations.

Peculiar border laws evolved, such as cross-border marriages being

forbidden, on pain of death, without the agreement of both wardens. The tradition of 'hot trod' allowed, to someone whose cattle had been stolen, six days in which to recover his property. To do this he had to carry a burning peat on the tip of a lance and announce his intentions with 'hue and cry, hound and horn'. This wouldn't offer him any special protection, and he might be robbed, beaten, captured, ransomed or killed, but at least everyone knew why he was passing through. Anyone fleeing for their life could seek sanctuary in a church, while anyone who had committed heinous crimes could seek absolution at a monastery on payment of a fee! Protection rackets operated, and the English language derives words such as 'blackmail' and 'bereaved' from this era.

The Allendale 'Tar Barling', when 'Old Year's Night' is celebrated with a stirring fire festival (Day 1)

The Borders saw centuries of complex and deadly feuding, sometimes between English and Scots, sometimes between neighbouring families, and sometimes between factions within the same family. The wardens had to deal with frequent 'bills' – or complaints – so 'truce days' were held every 40 days or so to resolve differences. It was often the case that someone might be hanged before their trial took place, and if rope was scarce, drowning would suffice! Imprisonment was rarely an option due to lack of facilities, though a prison was eventually built at Hexham. Gammel's Path, high in the Cheviot Hills, was one of the remote locations where 'truce days' were held.

The 16th century saw the peak period of reiving activity, when even the wardens were involved in the business of robbery and revenge. 'Moss troopers', as the reivers were sometimes known, rode stocky ponies for speed over rugged terrain, and wore rudimentary armour consisting of a steel helmet and leather jacket. For weapons they carried a lance and a sword, later supplemented with a pistol or two. After centuries of lawbreaking, hunting and being hunted, it was a way of life that people were born into.

In 1525 the Archbishop of Glasgow pronounced an exceedingly lengthy, and remarkably comprehensive, blood-curdling curse on Scottish reiver families (see Appendix 4). On the English side, the preacher Bernard

Gilpin spent his summers evangelising with great success among some of the roughest and toughest Northumberland communities, becoming known as the 'Apostle of the North'.

Following the Union of Crowns in 1603, England and Scotland suddenly found themselves ruled by the same monarch, in the person of James I of England and VI of Scotland. This paved the way for a complete cessation of hostilities between both nations, but initially had little effect where the reiver lifestyle was ingrained in the population. Drastic action was required, and even the use of the word 'Borders' was forbidden, being replaced by the term 'Middle Shires'. Families who refused to obey the law were rounded up and evicted, resettling in Ireland or North America. Those who accepted the law were rewarded with land, so that a measure of peace and prosperity settled on the region. The Union of the Parliaments was achieved in 1707, but the Borders saw a little more action during the Jacobite 'risings' of 1715 and 1745.

Rousing Borders ballads and the romantic stories penned by Sir Walter Scott cast a rosy hue on what must have been a most bloodthirsty period. One can only rejoice at the peace and tranquillity of the Northumberland countryside today, but also occasionally succumb to a few moments of melancholy while remembering the strife and senselessness of those troubled times.

Much marginal land in Northumberland is used for forestry plantations so expect some clear felling

GEOLOGY AND SCENERY

The oldest rocks in Northumberland are seldom seen, but underlie the whole region. They are Silurian slates and 'greywackes', around 420 million years old. The Cheviot Hills were formed of two igneous rock types in the Devonian period. A mass of andesite lavas make up almost all the lower foothills, dating back 395 million years. The central part of the Cheviot Hills is a huge dome of

17

granite, pushed up into the Earth's crust some 360 million years ago.

South of the Cheviot Hills, most of Northumberland is made up of Carboniferous rocks. These were laid down in a sea over 300 million years ago. At certain times the sea was fairly shallow and the water clear, so that corals flourished, and their remains formed limestone beds. At other times distant mountain ranges were being eroded, and rivers brought mud, sand and gravel into the sea, which formed great thicknesses of mudstone, sandstone and gritstone.

Sometimes the rivers formed vast deltas, which allowed strange, fern-like trees to gain rootholds, only to be toppled by floods and buried beneath more mud and sand. The plant matter was compressed over time to form coal measures. These are Northumberland's predominant rock types, forming rocky edges in some places, but breaking down to form sandy soils in others, with enough coal to support a little mining activity.

The Carboniferous rocks were laid down in layers, and that helps to explain what happened next, around 295 million years ago. A great mass of molten dolerite was squeezed, under enormous pressure, between the layers of rock – rather like jam between two slices of bread. This rock is always prominent wherever it outcrops, and is referred to as the Whin Sill. It forms some of Northumberland's most striking landscapes. The highest parts of Hadrian's Wall, for example, were

built along the crest of the Whin Sill, so as a geological feature it has shaped the political landscape of Britain! The Whin Sill outcrops all the way across Northumberland and is notable along the coast, where its higher parts are crowned with castles at Bamburgh and Lindisfarne, while its lower parts form low cliffs and the Farne Islands.

Almost 300 million years of geological time are 'missing' in Northumberland, so the rock types and formations are mostly very old. The region was scoured during the ice age, within the last couple of million years, and many parts are covered with glacial detritus, in the form of boulder clay, sand and gravel.

Today's visitor looks at the landscape to see the rounded, resistant humps of the Cheviot Hills, rocky gritstone edges on lower hills and moorlands, and the jagged crest of the Whin Sill often flanked by gentler countryside.

WILDLIFE

Northumberland is good cattle country, and cattle rearing, and cattle rustling naturally, is part of the region's heritage. In 1270 a herd of wild cattle was enclosed within parkland at Chillingham, and since then has had no interaction with other cattle, or much interaction with human beings either, so visitors can observe how the habits of the 'wild' Chillingham herd differ from those of domesticated cattle.

The Reivers Way runs almost all the way round Northumberland, which is excellent cattle country

Apart from farm stock, or feral goats in the Cheviot Hills, other large mammals that can be seen around Northumberland include shy roe deer, generally seen grazing the margins of forests at dawn and dusk, along with rabbits, foxes and badgers. Britain's most northerly colony of dormice are found at Allen Banks, and the elusive otter can be spotted, with patience, beside rivers, ponds or on the coast.

Reptiles are seldom seen, but adders and grass snakes are present, along with slow worms and common lizards. Amphibians such as frogs are more likely to be visible, while toads and newts are much less common.

The heather moorlands of Northumberland are managed for grouse shooting, and apart from large populations of red grouse, there are a few black grouse in the region. Late spring and early summer are important times for breeding birds. Cuckoos will be heard as they advance northwards, while skylark, lapwing, snipe and curlew are often seen on broad moorlands. The curlew is the emblem of the Northumberland National Park. Watch out for buzzards and kestrels in open areas. Herons fish in ponds and watercourses, while dippers and grey wagtails will completely submerge themselves in rivers.

On the coast, and more particularly on the Farne Islands, thousands of pairs of breeding birds fill every possible nook and cranny to rear their young. Most notable are the puffins, with guillemots, shags and razorbills also seen in great numbers. Raucous arctic and sandwich terns, kittiwakes

The emblem of the Northumberland National Park is a curlew, commonly seen and heard on the moorlands

and other members of the gull family are also present. The autumn and winter months are notable for an influx of wildfowl, especially around Budle Bay and Lindisfarne. Be ready for surprises – old gravel pits in Coquetdale have been transformed into wildlife habitats that are now popular with bird-watchers.

ACCESS LAND AND THE CROW ACT

When Harold Wade walked the Reivers Way in 1975, he didn't always follow rights of way. When James Roberts walked the route in 1992, he made sweeping changes to ensure

20

that rights of way were always followed. In a couple of instances, both Wade and Roberts followed roads when they could have used nearby rights of way. Things have changed over the years, and most rights of way are clearly signposted and waymarked. Indeed, a couple of places that once lacked rights of way now have them. Furthermore, large areas of open moorland have been designated 'access land' under the Countryside and Rights of Way (CROW) Act 2000. Routes that Wade 'trespassed' upon, and Roberts saw fit to avoid, are now available to walkers, and therefore included in this guidebook.

'Access land' should not be regarded as offering unlimited access. Some areas are indeed open all the time, but others are 'restricted', and can be closed for various reasons, including grouse shooting and the movement of animals. Access land on the Reivers Way will either be available to walkers all of the time, or at least most of the time, so it will usually be possible to stay high and follow Harold Wade's original route. Just in case the land is closed for any reason, the low-level detours made by Roberts serve as alternative routes. It is possible to check in advance whether access land is open or closed by going to www.countrysideaccess.gov.uk. It is also likely that notices will be posted at the main access points indicating the nature of any closures.

TRAVEL TO NORTHUMBERLAND

By Air

The most convenient airport for the Reivers Way is Newcastle Airport, tel 0871 8821121, www.newcastle airport.com, which has good connections with the rest of Britain, as well as several European cities. The Metro system links the airport with Newcastle Central Station every few minutes for onward travel.

By Sea

Ferries reach Newcastle from Amsterdam, bringing the Reivers Way within easy reach of the Low Countries. Check ferry schedules with DFDS Seaways, tel 0871 5229955, www. dfdsseaways.co.uk. DFDS runs its own buses between the ferryport and Newcastle Central Station for onward travel.

By Rail

Cross Country trains provides direct long-distance rail access to Newcastle and Alnmouth from Exeter, Bristol, Birmingham, Edinburgh and Glasgow, tel 0844 8110124, www. crosscountrytrains.co.uk. Newcastle also has direct National Express East Coast rail services from London Kings Cross and Edinburgh, www. nationalexpresseastcoast.com. Rail services between Carlisle and Newcastle are operated by Northern Rail, www. northernrail.org, which also operates between Alnmouth and Newcastle.

By Bus

National Express runs direct services from London Victoria Coach Station to Newcastle, as well as direct services from Edinburgh and Wrexham, passing through Otterburn, tel 0871 7818181, www. nationalexpress.com. Some long-distance Arriva buses operate to Newcastle, and the city is one of the hubs in their network, tel 0870 1201088, www.arrivabus.co.uk. Classic Coaches offer an interesting, regular cross-country service from Blackpool to Newcastle, www. classic-coaches.co.uk.

TRAVEL AROUND NORTHUMBERLAND

By Train

Regular daily trains from Newcastle serve the start and finish of the Reivers Way, Corbridge and Alnwick. Services from Newcastle to Corbridge are operated by Northern Rail, www. northernrail.org. Services from Alnmouth to Newcastle are operated by Cross Country trains, www.cross-countrytrains.co.uk, and Northern Rail, www.northernrail.org.

By Bus

Arriva North East provides the bulk of bus services out of Newcastle, www. arrivabus.co.uk. There are also half-a-dozen minor bus operators providing useful rural services around different parts of Northumberland, and these are mentioned in the guidebook where appropriate.

Traveline and Taxis

It can be frustrating trying to gather individual public transport leaflets, and there is no comprehensive public transport guide covering Northumberland. However, details of all modes of transport to the area can be checked with Transport Direct, www.transportdirect. info. Public transport in and around the county can be checked with Traveline North East, tel 0871 2002233, www. travelinenortheast.info. If a taxi is needed at any point and you don't have any local numbers, call the National Taxi Hotline – on 0800 654321 – and they will connect you with the nearest taxi in the scheme, so that you can negotiate a journey and check the price.

ACCOMMODATION

Organising lodgings on a long-distance walk requires a willingness to search diligently and juggle options to create

Some places have very little accommodation, such as Harbottle, which has only a single bed and breakfast (Day 6)

a workable schedule. Accommodation around Northumberland is unevenly spread, so while some places may have plenty of options, others have very little. Start by checking the most 'awkward' locations first, such as the remote farmhouse bed and breakfast at Uswayford (end of Day 6/start of Day 7), and work outwards from those places once you have secured a bed. Sheer pressure of walkers can affect all available lodgings near popular Hadrian's Wall. The coastal resort of Seahouses offers abundant accommodation, but it can be very busy in the summer.

In case of difficulty obtaining accommodation, a simple bus journey off-route may bring plenty more options within reach. If detours off-route are going to be made, then be sure to obtain the relevant bus timetables in advance, and build the necessary time into your schedule to leave and re-join the route. In some cases, nearby accommodation providers may be prepared to do pick-ups and drop-offs, but arrange this well in advance if required. If something prevents you from reaching accommodation that has been booked, call the proprietor at the earliest opportunity and explain. This might enable them to take another booking and avoid losing money, and if they know you are safe, they won't be worrying about you and possibly calling out the rescue services.

Places with lodgings are mentioned throughout this book, and a basic accommodation list is given in Appendix 2, but bear in mind that these things tend to change quite frequently. For up-to-date details of accommodation, check the *Northumberland Holiday and Short Breaks Guide*, which can be obtained free by calling 01670 794520 or visiting www.visitnorthumberland.com. The guide is available from tourist information centres, and in most cases such places will be able to advise and assist with booking accommodation, possibly saving many fruitless phone calls.

FOOD AND DRINK

While there are several shops, pubs, restaurants and cafés around the Reivers Way, they are very unevenly distributed. On some parts of the route there may be no refreshments available throughout the day, and if staying overnight at Uswayford (end of Day 6 and start of Day 7), evening meals should be ordered well in advance.

Never set out on any part of the Reivers Way without first noting the availability of food and drink for at least a couple of days in advance. Be sure to carry sufficient provisions to allow for lengthy gaps between shops, taking special note of the paucity of services in the broad and bleak Cheviot Hills.

Things change – Harold Wade noted services that were gone by the time James Roberts walked the route, and I in turn have noticed services that have disappeared, as well as completely new ones. In one instance I saw a pub in a village which, on my return a few months later, was closed. Be prepared for changes.

MONEY

While an increasing number of accommodation providers, shops, pubs and restaurants will take credit cards in payment, many don't, and walkers will need a certain amount of cash to cover goods and services while on the move, especially on the more remote parts of this trail. If unsure about carrying large amounts of cash, at least try and budget ahead, then be aware of any places along the way that have banks and ATMs. Many are mentioned in the route description, and some supermarkets offer a 'cashback' service.

TOURIST INFORMATION

- Corbridge, tel 01434 632815
- Hexham, tel 01434 652220
- Otterburn, tel 01830 520225
- Rothbury, tel 01669 620887
- Wooler, tel 01668 282123
- Seahouses, tel 01665 720884
- Craster, tel 01665 576007
- Alnwick, tel 01665 511333

PLANNING YOUR WALK

When to Walk

Spring can be a splendid time to walk the Reivers Way, when the countryside is bursting with new life. Lambs are suckling in the lower pastures, flowers rise from fields and roadside verges, and migrating birds arrive and sort out their nesting sites.

Walking in the winter months means limited daylight, but good progress is possible when wet ground freezes

The peak summer period offers the longest daylight hours and possibly the best weather. Lowland hayfields are mown to stubble, while heather moorlands turn purple and the bracken lies deep on the hillsides. Some heather moorland might be used for grouse shooting. Accommodation in popular places might be fully booked, but apart from that all services should be in full swing and ferries will be running to the Farne Islands.

Autumn is a time for harvesting crops, and the daylight hours begin to shorten, with the possibility of cooler and wetter weather.

The winter months occasionally feature sharp frosts, so that boggy parts freeze over, but prolonged wet weather, or rare falls of deep snow, can make this a difficult time to walk. Some of the businesses along the way, especially accommodation providers, close for the winter.

What the Walking's Like

Walking the Reivers Way is fairly straightforward, but bear in mind that the route is not specifically waymarked, although there are the usual public footpath and bridleway signposts and markers. Keep an eye on the route description and follow your progress on the map. Compared to many parts of the country, Northumberland's footpaths are lightly trodden, and there are often great distances between settlements and their facilities. Walkers will be encountered in popular places, such

as Allen Banks, Hadrian's Wall, the Simonside Hills, the Cheviot Hills and much of the Northumberland coast. At other times, you may walk all day without meeting any other walkers, even in the summer. The abiding memory is of a succession of scenic highlights separated by wide open, sparsely populated countryside.

Terrain

The Reivers Way includes gentle walks through river valleys and low-lying fields, but this can quickly give way to bleak and barren moorland or extensive forests. When walking far from habitation it is essential to take care over route-finding, as any unintended detours off-route will take time and energy to recover. When mist covers featureless moorlands, or when several junctions of forest tracks are encountered, it is worth taking time to pinpoint your position on a map, and then ensure that you head in the correct direction.

When there is a choice of routes available, study both options carefully, weighing their advantages and disadvantages and take the weather into account. There are two options between Elsdon and Rothbury (Day 5), and both of them include the Simonside Hills. Between Uswayford and Wooler (Day 7), the high-level route over the Cheviot is often easier to follow than the low-level alternative outflanking it. Once the Cheviot Hills are left behind, the route wanders through fields and low hills,

25

with variant routes reaching the Northumberland coast (Day 8). The coast (Day 9) features easy, low-level walking, despite the rugged little cliffs that are often in view. In a nutshell, the terrain along the Reivers Way is remarkably varied from day to day.

Daily Schedule

The Reivers Way can be walked in as little as a week by experienced long-distance walkers, but nine days is more practical, with two weeks offering a fairly leisurely approach. Bear in mind that there where alternative routes are available, distances and the nature of the terrain differ. Walkers shouldn't feel obliged to follow the nine-day schedule in this book too rigidly, but should adapt and amend it to suit their individual requirements. Trying to arrange a schedule to omit the solitary farmhouse bed and breakfast at Uswayford (end of Day 6 and start of Day 7), can be difficult, and this

is the sort of place where a carefully planned schedule can unravel if all the beds are taken.

Maps

Four Ordnance Survey Landranger maps cover the Reivers Way at a scale of 1:50,000. The relevant sheets are 75, 80, 81 and 87. Extracts from these maps are used throughout the guidebook, with an overview (pages 8 and 9) to show the full course of the Reivers Way. For greater detail, and to see the extent of designated access land, five Ordnance Survey Explorer maps cover the route at a scale of 1:25,000. The relevant sheets are OL16, OL42, OL43, 332 and 340.

How to Use this Guidebook

The main feature of this guidebook is a continuous route description, illustrated with OS map extracts. Alternative routes for Days 5, 7 and 8 are described at the end of the main route descriptions, with further OS

Waymarking and signposting on rights of way is usually quite good, but keep your eyes open for markers

map extracts showing the variant sections of route in blue.

Some daily stretches are longer than others, and there are long stretches without access to food, drink or accommodation. If a day's walk seems too long, then check to see whether it can be broken halfway, whether accommodation is available, and whether public transport allows a detour off-route.

Even when facilities are mentioned, bear in mind that they are subject to change. Hotels and bed and breakfasts may not always be open, and they may not always have a bed available, so it is wise to book in advance.

Food and drink may not be available on long stretches, so think twice before passing a shop or pub, and be sure to read ahead to discover where the next ones are located.

If relying on public transport to travel to and from various parts of the walk, check timetables in advance, using the contact details given in this guidebook. If you need specific, up-to-date information about facilities along the way, contact the relevant tourist information centres and ask for advice (see Appendix 3).

Equipment

If you are approaching the Reivers Way as a series of one-day walks, then all you need is your normal day pack, containing the usual waterproofs, food and drink for the day, small first aid kit, maps, compass – and the ability to use them.

If you are walking the route as a continuous long-distance trek and planning to use hotels and bed and breakfasts, then only a little more kit is needed. A complete change of clothes for the evenings is desirable, so that walking clothes can be washed and dried wherever facilities are available. It might be a good idea to pack a couple of spare pairs of socks, which could prove useful if crossing boggy ground in wet weather, day after day.

Campsites are infrequent along the Reivers Way, so if you do plan to carry a tent, sleeping bag and cooking equipment, then it is likely that at certain points you will need to 'wild camp'. Wherever possible, ask for permission, but if this isn't practical, then camp unobtrusively, pitching late and leaving early, taking care to leave absolutely no trace of your stay. If you are camping and cooking, then the availability of shops along the way needs to be borne in mind, and remember that the choice may be limited in a small village store.

RESCUE SERVICES

The emergency services – mountain rescue, police, ambulance, fire brigade or coastguard – are all alerted by dialling 999 (or the European 112). Be ready to supply full details of the nature of the emergency, so that an appropriate response can be made. Keep in contact with the emergency services in case they require further information or clarification.

DAY 1
Corbridge to Allendale Town

Start	Corbridge – NY989643
Finish	Allendale Town – NY836557
Distance	27.5km (17 miles)
Maps	OS Landranger 87 or OS Explorer OL43
Terrain	Fields, forests and riverside paths are followed by moorland tracks, including some that can be wet underfoot.
Refreshments	Plenty of choice at Corbridge. Pub off-route from Peth Foot. Plenty of choice at Allendale Town.
Public Transport	Regular daily trains, as well as Arriva and Stagecoach buses, serve Corbridge from Newcastle and Carlisle. The Hadrian's Wall bus serves Corbridge daily through the summer, linking with all parts of Hadrian's Wall, as well as Newcastle and Carlisle. Tynedale and Tyne Valley buses serve Allendale Town from Hexham daily, except Sundays.

As with any long-distance walk, the golden rule is not to burn yourself out on the first day. This is a long day's walk, with fiddly route-finding all the way through the valley of Devil's Water, followed by a long moorland crossing that can be wet and boggy on its higher parts. If it seems too much, then break the journey using one of three accommodation options before the halfway point, and cover this initial stage over two shorter days.

CORBRIDGE

Spend time in Corbridge before starting the Reivers Way – if possible try to arrive in the afternoon and stay for the night, or at least arrive early in the day just to be able to stroll round the streets before leaving.

When the Romans pushed Dere Street north through Northumberland, they crossed the River Tyne near Corbridge, linking with the coast-to-coast Stanegate. The Roman fort of Corstopitum stands at the junction of these two roads, pre-dating Hadrian's

*The parish church in the middle of
Corbridge – a village that has seen
centuries of warfare and strife*

Wall. There is a splendid museum on site, as well as a café. There is an entry charge, and the site is open daily from April to October, and at week-ends through the winter, tel 01434 632349, www. english-heritage.org.uk.

The fort guarded the Roman bridge, though masonry from the bridge is now inconveniently located on the opposite bank of the river. The river has shifted since the bridge was built, and to spare the massive stone building blocks from damage, they were lifted, moved and rebuilt away from the riverbank.

There are plenty of fine old buildings around Corbridge, such as St Andrew's church, with the Vicar's Pele Tower alongside. There is another pele tower where the old Newcastle road leaves town, built into Low Hall. These towers are features of reiver country – places where cattle could easily be driven inside on the ground floor, while people took refuge above in time of strife.

There was plenty of strife in this area. Ethelred, King of Northumbria, was slain here in 796AD, and it is also where Regnald the Dane defeated both English and Scots armies in 918AD. King David I of Scotland occupied the town in 1138, while King John sacked it in 1201. Corbridge suffered three burnings, by William Wallace in 1296, Robert the Bruce in 1312, and King David II in 1346.

There is accommodation in Corbridge, plenty of pubs and restaurants, shops, a post office, two banks and an ATM. The tourist information centre, tel 01434 632815, offers a leaflet called 'A Walk of Discovery around Corbridge'.

Leave **Corbridge** by heading downhill from the Angel Inn,

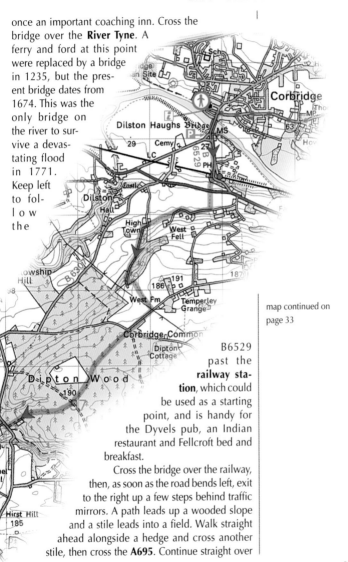

once an important coaching inn. Cross the bridge over the **River Tyne**. A ferry and ford at this point were replaced by a bridge in 1235, but the present bridge dates from 1674. This was the only bridge on the river to survive a devastating flood in 1771. Keep left to follow the

map continued on page 33

B6529 past the **railway station**, which could be used as a starting point, and is handy for the Dyvels pub, an Indian restaurant and Fellcroft bed and breakfast.

Cross the bridge over the railway, then, as soon as the road bends left, exit to the right up a few steps behind traffic mirrors. A path leads up a wooded slope and a stile leads into a field. Walk straight ahead alongside a hedge and cross another stile, then cross the **A695**. Continue straight over a stile to follow another field path, crossing a stile to reach a quiet road. Turn right along this road and follow it almost to **West Fell**, where it becomes a private drive.

Continue straight along an enclosed path and later go through a gate. Follow a grassy path flanked by gorse and thorns, keeping well to the left of **High Town**. Go through a gate and follow a track away from the farm, but turn left up a path on a wooded slope.

Keep to the edge of the wood, watching for pheasants and deer, and avoid a couple of lesser paths climbing to the left. The path climbs more steeply and bends left to reach the top of a plantation. Turn right through a gate and walk alongside a wall. Pass through two large fields, converging with a pylon line to reach a gate and a road near **West Farm**.

Turn right along the road to reach a junction where a grassy patch sits in the road. Keep straight ahead as signposted for Lightwater Cottages, following a grassy path between forest plots of different ages. Note the parallel lines of tumbled drystone walls, which the path follows faithfully through **Dipton Wood**. ◄

Enough light reaches the forest floor for it to support plenty of heather and bilberry.

Cross over a prominent track around 190m (625ft) and keep straight ahead along another track as marked. Climb a little, then descend, and the path is worn deeply into creamy, soft sandstone. When Lightwater Cottages are reached, walk down the access road to reach the **B6306**.

Nunsbrough Wood is managed by the Woodland Trust, while a nearby wildflower meadow is designated access land.

Turn right up the road, then left as signposted for Ordley, passing through a stone gateway and following an access road down to a stud farm at **Linnel**. Keep right of all the buildings and go through a gate into a field. Look across the field to spot another gate, where a track leads down a wooded slope. Cross a footbridge over **Devil's Water**, then climb up stone steps to reach a track.

The Travellers Rest lies uphill off-route, offering food, drink and accommodation.

Turn right to follow the track a little downhill, then uphill. ◄ Turn left down a path to enter the meadow at a gate and stile, turning right to follow a path through it. Cross a little footbridge and walk upstream beside Devil's Water, towards a fine house and garden at **Peth Foot**. Before reaching the house, turn left to cross a footbridge. ◄

map continued
on page 34

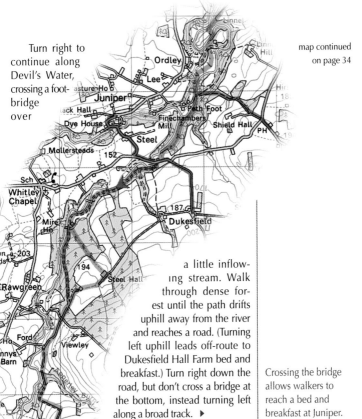

Turn right to continue along Devil's Water, crossing a foot-bridge over a little inflowing stream. Walk through dense forest until the path drifts uphill away from the river and reaches a road. (Turning left uphill leads off-route to Dukesfield Hall Farm bed and breakfast.) Turn right down the road, but don't cross a bridge at the bottom, instead turning left along a broad track. ▶

Again, the route traces Devil's Water upstream through a wooded valley, passing a curious ruin that was once a smelt mill. The track later leaves the forest and heads through fields to reach a house at Redlead Mill. Walk straight past the house and through a gate to continue further upstream.

The track ahead was used by both Wade and Roberts, but is not a right of way. It leads further upstream, then pulls away from the river and climbs to a bend on a quiet road near **Viewley**.

Crossing the bridge allows walkers to reach a bed and breakfast at Juniper.

33

map continued from
page 33

To stay on rights of way, however, turn left after leaving Redlead Mill and follow the track away from the river, then head right along a forest path. Continue up through fields and keep left of the farm buildings at **Steel Hall**. Turn right to follow a track past the farm and across fields to pass a solitary byre. Enter a forest and walk straight ahead to reach the bend on the road near **Viewley**. Continue straight along and down the road to reach a hairpin bend. Turn left along the access road for Embley, which rises gently, drops down to Devil's Water, then climbs up a wooded slope. Follow the access track up between fields then turn right to go straight through the farmyard at **Embley**. Watch for a gate on the right on leaving the farmyard, which bears a bridleway marker.

A track runs downhill, then bear left a little to spot a marker post in a gap between two holly trees. Pass this and look down across a rushy slope to spot a stile. A path leads down stone steps from here to a footbridge spanning **Devil's Water**.

Don't cross the footbridge, but follow a rugged path upstream. Drift away from the river, passing through a couple of gates in fences, climbing uphill and crossing a stile near a corner on a fence. Next, traverse across a couple of fields, passing through gates, to find a muddy track leading down to the farm of **Burntshield Haugh**. Cross a concrete bridge over Devil's Water one last time and follow a concrete farm road uphill.

Go through a gate and walk further up the access track, but don't follow it when it turns right. Instead, cross a stile and walk up through a field to cross another stile. Walk up towards **Hesleywell**. Turn left to walk away from the farm, then watch for a couple of stone step-stiles to keep just to the left of **New House**. A couple of ladder-stiles are crossed, and the idea is to aim to the right of the farm buildings at **Long Lee** to reach its access road.

Cross over the road and go through a gate, then climb diagonally through a rugged field and pass through little gates in front of the house at **Steel**. Watch for a gate on the way through fields beyond, and keep to the right of the farmhouse at **Stobby Lea**. Walk down through fields to cross a footbridge, then climb to reach **Harwood Shield**, going straight through the farmyard and passing substantial stone outbuildings.

Turn left along the farm access road,

35

Looking back along the Reivers Way, from Stobbs Cross towards the heather moors of Hexhamshire Common

The broad moorlands of Hexhamshire Common are designated access land, and used for grouse shooting.

then right along a clear track that passes some walled and fenced enclosures on the moorland. ◄

After passing the last enclosure, turn right and follow a track down through a gate and across **Stobbylee Burn**. Climb steeply up a stony track to reach a junction on **Hangman Hill**.

Turn left downhill, then the track swings right to reach a junction of tracks beside a stone bridge spanning **Black Sike**. Turn left to cross the bridge, and follow the track past a corrugated black shooting hut. When a complex junction of tracks is reached before a building at **Ladle Well**, simply turn right up a rutted moorland track. This track climbs parallel to a drystone wall, drops to cross a stream, then climbs again to **Stobb Cross** at 401m (1316ft).

Cross a track here and keep straight ahead for Allendale, bearing in mind that the moorland path can be wet and boggy. The track runs down through a gate and passes between fields before suddenly landing on a road near **the Spittal**. Both Wade and Roberts advised walkers to follow the road down to Allendale Town, but a field path can be found by following the access road for **High Scotch Halls Farm**, offering a much better finish to the day.

Pass the farm, cross a stone step-stile on the left, and head diagonally right across a field to cross another step-stile. Pass in front of a house and follow its access track, then cross another step-stile on the left. Walk to a brow offering a fine view of Allendale, then walk downhill and cross an access road.

Drift right to go through a gateway between two fields, then head for the far corner of a field to cross a step-stile. Cross one last stile on the way downhill, then squeeze between two houses and head straight into **Allendale Town**.

ALLENDALE TOWN

Allendale Town, formerly known as Allenton, was granted a charter by Edward I. Lead mining was an important industry, but the ore contained a significant amount of silver. In the mid-19th century the population expanded and a smelt mill was constructed in the dale. Noxious fumes were conducted uphill through stone-built flues to be vented high on the moors.

New Year's Eve is referred to as Old Year's Night in Allendale, and the local folk celebrate it with a stirring fire festival. Tough-looking Dalesfolk don fancy dress and are known as 'guisers'. They carry blazing tar barrels on their heads and process round town, hurling the barrels onto a central bonfire as the church bells ring in the New Year. After frantically 'first footing' round all the houses, the local folk melt away, leaving hordes of visiting tourists wondering what happened! Be warned that not a bed is to be had in the area during 'tar-barling'.

Allendale Town has broad greens, a range of accommodation, a few shops, pubs, restaurants and cafés. The post office has an ATM and there is a bank. Tynedale and Tyne Valley buses run to and from Hexham, except Sundays.

DAY 2
Allendale Town to Bardon Mill

Start	Allendale Town – NY836557
Finish	Bardon Mill – NY781645
Distance	17.5km (11 miles)
Maps	OS Landranger 87 or OS Explorer OL43
Terrain	Mostly riverside paths, fields and woodlands. Some paths are steep and rugged.
Refreshments	Pub off-route at Carts Bog. Pub at Bardon Mill.
Public Transport	Regular daily trains, and Arriva and Stagecoach buses, link Bardon Mill with Hexham, Newcastle and Carlisle.

This is a relatively short and easy day's walk, and mostly confined to the valley of the River Allen. There are plenty of riverside paths, but every so often there is a diversion away from the flow. The highlight of the day is deep, well-wooded Staward Gorge and Allenbanks. The end of the day is at Bardon Mill, though strong walkers might like to press on towards Hadrian's Wall.

Follow a road downhill to leave **Allendale Town**, passing the Hare and Hounds pub. A path short-cuts a road bend, but watch for another path on the right, signposted for Oakpool. The walk downstream beside the **River East Allen** is quite popular.

Pass an old mine building and note the stream flowing from a level with a grille across it. Further along the wooded path a stone abutment once supported a railway bridge linking Allendale with Hexham.

Turn left to follow the **B6295** across a twin-arched bridge. Turn right as signposted for Oakpool to follow a rugged riverside path across a wooded slope. Leave the woods to continue through meadows, where the path becomes vague.

When a track is reached, follow it straight towards an **isolated house**. Keep well to the left just before the house,

then watch for a stile on the right to head back to the house. Turn left to cross a footbridge over a stream. Continue

map continued on page 42

downstream through a meadow and cross a stone stile, followed by a footbridge called Maggies Bridge.

Keep right to walk a short way through woods, then a field, to reach another solitary house at **Kiddygreen**. Follow the access road away from the house to reach **Oakpool Farm**. ▶

Turn left along a road, still heading downstream, then climb steeply from the river up a wooded slope. Turn right down a farm access road, but before reaching the buildings at **Hindley Hill**, go through a gate on the left. Walk alongside a double-fenced new hedgerow then go through a gate as marked.

Turn right alongside another double-fenced new hedgerow and go through another gate. Turn left to cross a muddy dip and walk along a grassy brow. Drop downhill beside a fence to find a gate at the bottom. Cross a broad bridge over the river to reach the farm of **Wide Eals**.

Follow the access road uphill from the farm to reach a tight bend on the **A686**. Turn left to follow the road down towards triple-arched **Cupola Bridge**, an 18th-century structure named after a nearby smelt mill, close

Should you need it, Struthers Farm bed and breakfast is across the bridge and up the hill from here.

Limestone pavement exposed in the bed
of the River Allen, as seen from the stone-
arched Cupola Bridge

to the confluence of the River East Allen and River West Allen.

Don't cross the bridge, but go through a gate to follow a path downstream by the **River Allen**. This path eventually ends among mossy boulders, so watch carefully to spot another path climbing steeply up a slope of beech and Scots pines. Pass a National Trust sign for Staward Gorge, and another one is passed at the top of the path.

STAWARD GORGE

Steep-sided Staward Gorge is a National Trust property. The woodlands are undoubtedly ancient, but non-native beeches and conifers have been planted. There is a long-term plan to fell most non-native trees and replant native species. The ground cover in the ancient parts includes moscatel, wood fescue, woodruff and hard shield fern. Woodland birds include tawny owls, wood warblers and willow tits. The river supports dippers, grey wagtails, goosanders and oystercatchers. The UK's most northerly colony of dormice lives in the gorge, while with patience an otter might be spotted.

Cross a stile into a rough-pasture field and turn left. Follow the edge of the field to a stile and step onto the **A686** again. Turn left to follow the road past an enormous stone wall to reach Staward Station (weekend bed and breakfast available) on the old Hexham to Allendale railway. ▶

Go through a gate on the left, as signposted, and walk down through rough pasture. Go through another gate and climb gently to a ruin called **Gingle Pot**, formerly a cattle drovers' inn. Go through a gateway and follow a drystone wall roughly northwards. A grassy path runs alongside, while the rest of the field is rushy.

The path runs towards a forest then splits into two. Take the path on the left, gently downhill to a gate where there is a National Trust sign for Staward Gorge. The path runs along a narrow, steep-sided, well-wooded ridge between Allendale and Harsondale, reaching the ruins of Staward Peel.

The Carts Bog Inn is further along the main road if food or drink is required.

41

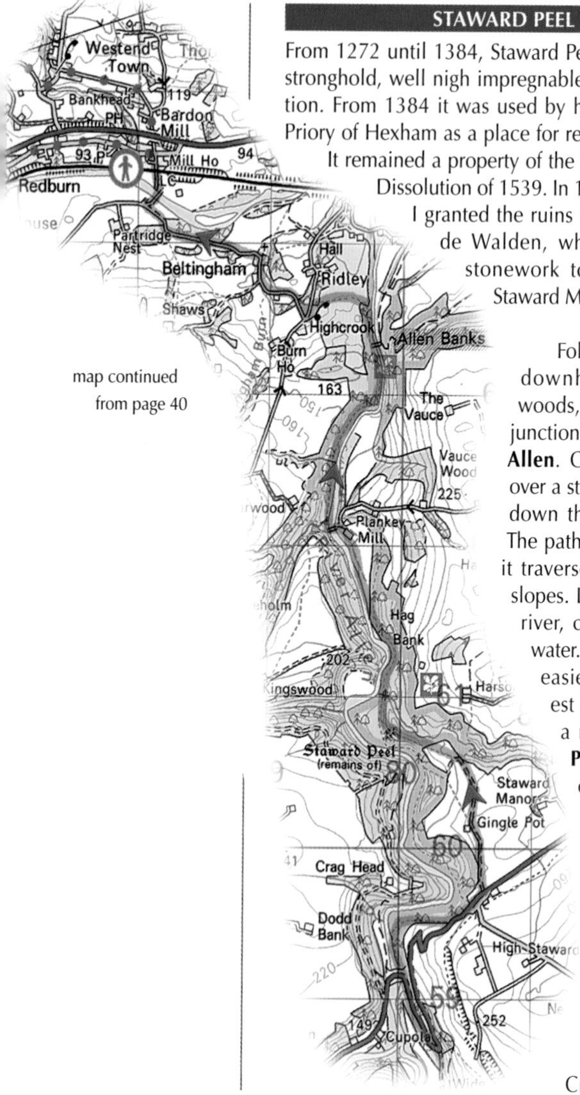

map continued
from page 40

map continued
from page 40

STAWARD PEEL

From 1272 until 1384, Staward Peel was a border stronghold, well nigh impregnable in such a location. From 1384 it was used by hermits from the Priory of Hexham as a place for retreat and prayer. It remained a property of the Church until the Dissolution of 1539. In 1613, King James I granted the ruins to Lord Howard de Walden, who stripped the stonework to build nearby Staward Manor.

Follow a path steeply downhill into denser woods, turning right at a junction to reach the **River Allen**. Cross a footbridge over a stream and continue down through the valley. The path can be rugged as it traverses steep, wooded slopes. Looking across the river, cliffs rise from the water. The path becomes easier, leaves the forest and runs through a meadow to reach **Plankey Mill** (basic campsite).

A suspension footbridge once spanned the River Allen here, but it was dismantled, and a new girder-and-wood bridge built nearby. Cross over it and

turn right to cross a smaller footbridge over a stream. Enter the little **Briarwood Banks** Nature Reserve, which is an ancient oak and ash wood, with some hazel coppice. A National Trust sign for **Allen Banks** is passed as the path continues downstream.

Walkers make their way across fields from the old Staward Station to the ruins of Staward Pele

ALLEN BANKS

Like Staward Gorge, Allen Banks is ancient woodland with some secondary plantings. Susan Davidson, who was related to the Bowes-Lyon family, lived at Ridley Hall in the mid-19th century. She oversaw the creation of a network of 'wilderness walks' in the wooded gorge at Allen Banks. Trees were hacked back and paths were laid, along with stone steps and strategically sited summerhouses. The estate was donated to the National Trust by Francis Bowes-Lyon in 1942. It is the only National Trust property of any size in the North Pennines. If there is time to spare, feel free to explore any of the other paths in the valley, though few of them are recorded on maps.

The broad and bouldery River Allen at Allen Banks, before it passes Ridley Hall

Heavy metals, such as lead and zinc from North Pennine mines, have poisoned the soil, so that Alpine penny-cress and spring sandwort find conditions to their liking.

The riverside path is quite easy, then it passes a sheer cliff of sandstone and enters a more restrictive part of the gorge. Pass a suspension footbridge, then watch carefully on the left to spot a flight of stone steps climbing up the wooded slope.

Cross a path at the top and also cross a stile to enter a field. Follow the course of an old 'ha-ha' wall, now accompanied by a fence, catching a glimpse of nearby **Ridley Hall**. When the wall peters out, go through a gate into a wood and keep straight ahead to reach a road.

Turn left along the road, then right at a nearby junction, to walk through the lovely, stone-built village of **Beltingham**, with its fine little church. Continue along the road to pass a nature reserve based on polluted ground. ◄

Paths can be used through the wooded reserve, otherwise follow the road. Eventually, a narrow footbridge spans the **River South Tyne**. Cross it, and also a level-crossing, then climb straight into the village of **Bardon Mill**.

BARDON MILL

The 17th-century woollen mill in the middle of the village was converted into a pottery in 1878 by Robert Errington and William Reay. They specialised in drainage pipes and sanitary ware, while today the roaring kilns turn out chunky garden planters and ornaments, www.erringtonreay.co.uk. A handful of small coal mines operated around the village in the 19th and 20th centuries. Facilities in the village include the Bowes Hotel, accommodation and a post office shop. Regular daily buses and trains allow easy links with nearby Hexham and Haltwhistle, as well as all points to Newcastle and Carlisle.

ROMAN VINDOLANDA

The Roman fort of Vindolanda lies off-route between Bardon Mill and Twice Brewed and might be visited by any walkers reaching Bardon Mill around lunch-time. The site dates largely from the third and fourth centuries, comprising a Roman fort and adjacent civilian settlement. An open-air museum features reconstructions of buildings and Hadrian's Wall. There is a café on site, tel 01434 344277, www.vindolanda.com. The Hadrian's Wall bus serves Vindolanda, but doesn't link with Bardon Mill. Maple Lodge is the nearest bed and breakfast.

DAY 3
Bardon Mill to Wark

Start	Bardon Mill – NY781645
Finish	Wark – NY860770
Distance	21km (13 miles)
Maps	OS Landranger 87 or OS Explorer OL43
Terrain	Moorland paths can be vague and need care. Also some fiddly field paths between farms.
Refreshments	Housesteads visitor centre kiosk. Old Repeater Station Café off-route from Sewing Shields. Pubs at Wark.
Public Transport	The Hadrian's Wall Bus links Housesteads with Carlisle and Newcastle daily through the summer. Tynedale buses serve Wark from Hexham and Bellingham daily, except Sundays.

Although this day seems relatively short and easy, Hadrian's Wall and Housesteads Roman Fort are intensely absorbing and occur before this stage is even half completed. If you want to explore thoroughly, then split the day and stay overnight nearby, bearing in mind that the Hadrian's Wall boasts a busy national trail, and accommodation comes under considerable pressure. The continuation to Wark crosses quiet and unfrequented moorland and fields.

Leave **Bardon Mill** by following the road signposted for Thorngrafton, heading uphill and passing beneath the busy **A69 bypass**. Turn right at a junction, again signposted for Thorngrafton, and climb steeply to a road junction at **Westend Town**. Turn left and head downhill towards a farm, but turn right up a track before reaching it. This grassy, walled track runs uphill, down across a dip, then uphill again to reach the moorland slopes of **Thorngrafton Common**.

Turn right, then quickly left, to follow a grassy ribbon of a path up a rushy slope. When the path forks, head left and keep climbing. The path becomes a rough-vegetated groove flanked by rushes, bracken or heather. Pass a marker post and climb to a very slight gap on the moorland crest, well to the left of a trig point at 279m (915ft). Even further left is the **Long Stone**, an ancient marker that is worth a short detour.

Pass through an old gateway in a drystone wall and head downhill, aiming for a road junction. Go through a gate to reach the junction, then turn right – or turn left to inspect the nearby

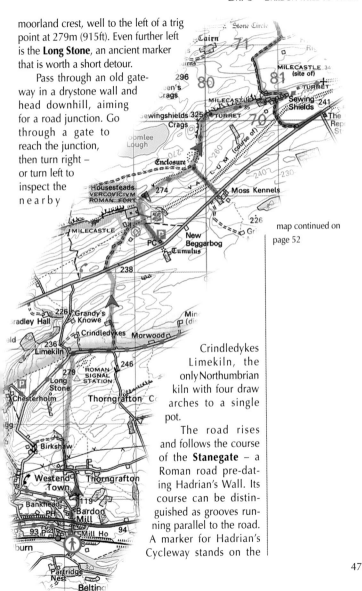

map continued on page 52

Crindledykes Limekiln, the only Northumbrian kiln with four draw arches to a single pot.

The road rises and follows the course of the **Stanegate** – a Roman road pre-dating Hadrian's Wall. Its course can be distinguished as grooves running parallel to the road. A marker for Hadrian's Cycleway stands on the highest point of the road. Further along the road, turn left down a farm access road, crossing a dip and climbing to **Crindledykes**.

Keep to the right of the farm, dropping down through two gates before climbing as marked over a grassy crest. Aim directly north to reach a gate leading onto the **B6318**, or Military Road. Go through a gate on the other side to follow an access road to **Housesteads**.

HOUSESTEADS ROMAN FORT

This site has a long and complex history, with some notable gaps. Bronze Age farming settlements were cleared during the construction of Hadrian's Wall. The *Augustan History* notes that the Romans decided 'to build the Wall, 80 miles long, to separate the Romans from the barbarians'. The fort at Housesteads, known to the Romans as Vercovicium, was probably garrisoned by 500 men. The fort was abandoned at the end of the fourth century and no one seems to have occupied the buildings afterwards.

The Venerable Bede noted 'it is eight feet in breadth, and twelve in height; and, as can be clearly seen to this day, ran straight from east to west'. There is no evidence of settlement at Housesteads until 1326, and even then there were only summer shielings. Permanent settlement was probably inadvisable due to border strife. Interest in the wall increased from 16th century, due in part to the curiosity generated by William Camden's *Britannia*. He didn't visit Housesteads, declaring 'I would not with safetie take the full survey of it for the rankie-robbers thereabouts'. General Wade's construction of the Military Road in the 1750s made Hadrian's Wall more accessible. Unfortunately, he destroyed much of the masonry to lay the foundations of his road, but some of the 'best bits' remain around Housesteads.

In 1801, at the age of 78, William Hutton explored Hadrian's Wall in a remarkable 600 mile

Hadrian's Wall and the ridge of the Whin Sill seen from the North Gate of Housesteads Roman Fort

(965km) round trip on foot from Birmingham. The Rev John Hodgson published the first detailed description of the wall in 1840. The archaeologist J Collingwood Bruce led the first 'pilgrimage' along the wall in 1849, and such 'pilgrimages' continue to this day. Some excavation work was done at Housesteads in 1849, but work to restore Hadrian's Wall commenced in earnest from 1908. Housesteads fort was given to the National Trust by JM Clayton in 1930, and it has since acquired other properties in the area.

Some 20 miles (32km) of the best stretches of Hadrian's Wall were included in the Northumberland National Park when it was designated 1956. After a lengthy period of consultation, the course of Hadrian's Wall was designated as a national trail in the year 2000 and is also a world heritage site.

There is a museum at Housesteads, with an admission charge to visit the ruins. A path leads down to the main road, where there is a visitor centre, refreshment kiosk, and the Hadrian's Wall Bus linking all points of Roman interest between Wallsend, Newcastle, Carlisle and Bowness-on-Solway. There is accommodation at nearby Beggar Bog, Moss Kennels and the Old Repeater Station, the last one having a café, but all of them are popular with people walking Hadrian's Wall.

If not visiting the interior of the fort, note that the land outside the walls is access land, allowing close-up views of the exterior. Simply walk round the perimeter wall of the fort and head down to a gap to cross Knag Burn.

KNAG BURN GATEWAY

Gateways were rarely constructed along Hadrian's Wall, with north–south traffic and trade largely regulated through forts or milecastles. This gateway was built in the fourth century, and featured double gates flanked by guardrooms.

Follow the course of Hadrian's Wall uphill, crossing a stile to enter a wood, and leaving the wood at a higher stile. ▶

Go down to a gap, then climb steeply uphill, down to another gap, then uphill again. There are fine views of Broomlee Lough and the Whin Sill ridge that bears Hadrian's Wall. The parallel earthworks of the Vallum, an earlier Roman frontier, are best viewed when the sun is low.

Drop down to a broad gap and cross a stile beside a gate, then climb onto **Sewingshields Crag**, where a trig point stands at 325m (1066ft). Some good fragments of Hadrian's Wall run across the top of the crag. Pass the square base of Turret 35a, followed later by the base of Milecastle 35.

The wall alongside is not Hadrian's Wall, but was built much later on its foundations using pillaged stone. Note the regular shapes of the stones, which match those seen earlier near Housesteads.

MILECASTLE 35

Milecastles were built every Roman mile, with turrets every third of a mile between them. The numbering system runs from east to west and is an invention of modern archaeologists, since no one knows whether the Romans had names for them. A gaming board was discovered at this milecastle. The site was used as a shieling in the 13th century, but abandoned by the 15th century.

Go through a gate into Sewingshields Wood, which is Scots pine and beech. Pass to the left of **Sewing Shields Farm** and leave the wood by another gate to reach a farm access road. Turn sharp left down the farm access road, turning right to follow it over rough pasture. The road turns right again and runs towards a farm called **Town Shields**. However, well before that point, turn left down a lesser track as marked by a post, and cross a bridge over Crook Burn.

Climb gently up a grassy track and go through a gate. Cross a grassy rise and note Folly Lake, surrounded by forest, on the left, with the dam of **Halleypike Lough** on moorland to the right. Go through another gate and follow the grassy track to a remote farmstead at **Stell Green**.

Take great care with route-finding over **Haughton Common** in poor visibility on the next stretch. Keep to the right of Stell Green to find a stile over a fence. Follow another fence to a corner and drift uphill to the right, passing a marker post.

map continued on page 53

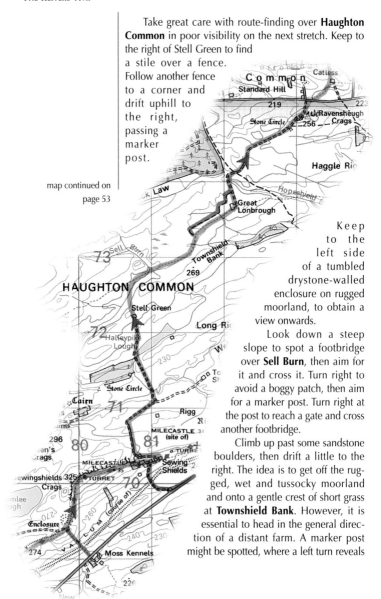

Keep to the left side of a tumbled drystone-walled enclosure on rugged moorland, to obtain a view onwards.

Look down a steep slope to spot a footbridge over **Sell Burn**, then aim for it and cross it. Turn right to avoid a boggy patch, then aim for a marker post. Turn right at the post to reach a gate and cross another footbridge.

Climb up past some sandstone boulders, then drift a little to the right. The idea is to get off the rugged, wet and tussocky moorland and onto a gentle crest of short grass at **Townshield Bank**. However, it is essential to head in the general direction of a distant farm. A marker post might be spotted, where a left turn reveals a grassy track crossing a boggy dip, then running parallel to a drystone wall.

Turn right to go through a gate in the wall, then walk straight towards the farm of **Great Lonbrough**. Keep to the right of the farmhouse, then go through a gate into the farmyard and leave along the access road. ▸

The farm road is plain and obvious as it wanders over the moors towards **Ravensheugh Crags**. Just before reaching the crags, a tiny stone circle containing only four boulders might be noticed up to the right.

The farm road reaches a minor road at the Manor House. Turn right along the road, then left over two drystone walls as indicated by a signpost.

Walk down a field to enter and leave a stand of pines by using stiles. Climb past the farm of **Catless** and cross a ladder-stile. Walk down a thistly field and watch for a couple of marker posts, swinging right at the bottom to follow **Gofton Burn** to a road.

Turn left along the road, then right across a stile, then cross a footbridge. Head downstream to pass a house at Shielahaugh, but later climb away from the stream before it enters a narrow,

If you don't like farmyards, walk parallel to the drystone wall long before reaching the farm, which is all on access land, and join the access road to the left of the farm.

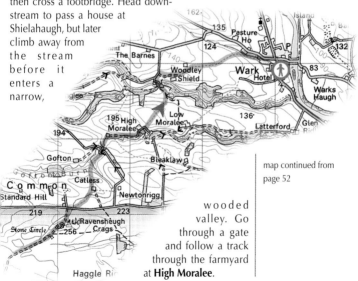

map continued from page 52

wooded valley. Go through a gate and follow a track through the farmyard at **High Moralee**.

Walk down the access road only until it bends right. Go through a gate and look up a grassy slope to spot a stile over a fence linking a line of trees. Continue over a grassy rise, then go down to a stile where a wall meets a fence. Follow the wall downhill, crossing it using a ladder-stile at a gateway, then head for the end of the wall. Turn left down a muddy slope, linking with a track that leads down to Ramshaw Mill and **Warks Burn**.

Cross a bridge over the river, then turn right up steps to go through a small gate. Walk as directed up a rough pasture and turn right to follow a track towards a farm at **Woodley Shield**. Cross a stile near the farm and follow marker posts uphill, keeping to the right of a large barn. Turn right to walk alongside fields as marked, and the path eventually runs down to a road. Turn right to follow the road into the village of **Wark**.

The village of Wark has a broad central green dominated by a huge horse chestnut tree

WARK-ON-TYNE

Wark-on-Tyne is a village of stout stone cottages built partly around a staggered crossroads and partly around a fine green dominated by a huge

horse chestnut. In the 12th century Wark was held by Scottish kings and, as the capital of the Lordship of Tynedale, was the administrative centre for a huge area. In 1715 Wark was part of the Earl of Derwentwater's estate and was forfeit, along with his life, when he supported the Jacobite rising that year. In the 19th century the Duke of Northumberland presided over the peculiarly named 'Wark Court Leet and View of Frankpledge'. A fine building, easily mistaken for a town hall, was built in 1874 facing the village green.

Facilities in Wark include the Battlesteads Hotel, Black Bull, Grey Bull, a post office shop and a butcher. Unless you are prepared to detour off-route for supplies, there are no more shops for the next two days, until Rothbury. Tynedale buses run daily, except Sundays, to Bellingham and Hexham.

DAY 4
Wark to Elsdon

Start	Wark – NY860770
Finish	Elsdon – NY935932
Distance	29km (18 miles)
Maps	OS Landrangers 80 and 87 or OS Explorers OL42 and OL43
Terrain	Mostly moorland and forests. Some good farm tracks, but also rugged moorland paths or stretches without paths.
Refreshments	The Tone Inn offers Sunday lunches. Elsdon has a pub and a tea room.
Public Transport	Snaith's buses link the Tone Inn with Otterburn and Hexham on weekdays. Snaith's also link Otterburn and Newcastle daily, except Sundays, and may divert to Elsdon on request. National Express runs a daily coach service through Otterburn, linking Newcastle and Edinburgh. Munro's of Jedburgh does the same, except Sundays. Arriva buses runs a Sunday service linking Otterburn with Keilder, Newcastle and Hexham.

Facilities are particularly sparse on this stretch of the route. Apart from Sunday lunches at the Tone Inn, there is nowhere offering food and drink. Fields, forests and broad moorlands are crossed one after the other until the lovely little village of Elsdon is reached. Services are fairly limited here, and it might be necessary to head off-route to Otterburn, in which case you need to check the limited public transport, or sort out a lift with an accommodation provider.

Leave **Wark** and its green to walk down to the **River North Tyne**. Cross a narrow girder-work bridge, dating from 1878, supported on seven stone piers. It replaced an earlier wooden bridge and an even earlier ferry. Turn left at a road junction as signposted for Birtley.

Turn right to climb from the river, then right again as signposted for Birtley. The road later climbs over a bridge on the old **North Tyne Railway**, which ran from 1856 to

1956, then crosses a dip. As the road climbs again, watch for a gate and a footpath signpost on the left. Walk up the grassy slope, then cross a dip.

Keep left of a stand of Scots pines to climb uphill, then head down to cross a stream and a stile. On the next climb, keep left of a house to follow a narrow, fenced path to a road near St Giles' church. Turn left to follow the road through the attractive and flowery village of **Birtley**, once the site of Birtley Pele.

Leave the village and take the second signposted road on the left, which is also used by the Reivers Cycleway. Follow the road, then cross a ladder-stile on the right. Two footpaths are signposted, and neither is visible on the ground. Take the one to the right, signposted for Pittland Hills, heading in the direction indicated across grassy moorland.

The way is later flanked by low, grassy embankments. A fenced field appears on the left, and it needs to be crossed diagonally using two stiles. Next, aim well to the left of the farm of **Pittland Hills** to find a gate leading onto a road.

Leaving Wark, a bridge built in 1878, replacing an earlier bridge and a ferry, spans the River North Tyne

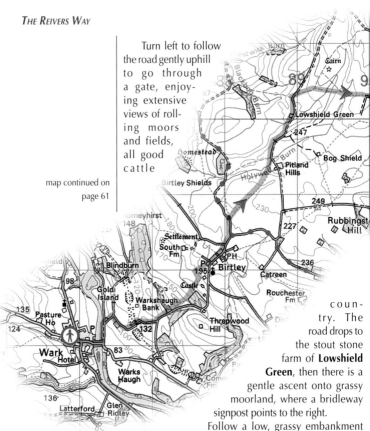

Turn left to follow the road gently uphill to go through a gate, enjoying extensive views of rolling moors and fields, all good cattle

map continued on page 61

country. The road drops to the stout stone farm of **Lowshield Green**, then there is a gentle ascent onto grassy moorland, where a bridleway signpost points to the right.

Follow a low, grassy embankment over the moor, but drift left from it later to follow quad-bike wheel-marks across a boggy dip. Climb a short way to cross a very gentle gap and pass a marker post. Head for a drystone wall and go through a gate, then climb gently to find another gate where a wall meets a fence.

Follow a track down through a farmyard, then follow the access road away from **Tone Hall**, which is rather like a tree-lined avenue. The busy **A68** is reached, based on the old Roman road of Dere Street, beside **the Tone Inn**. Sunday lunches are served, and there are occasional weekday

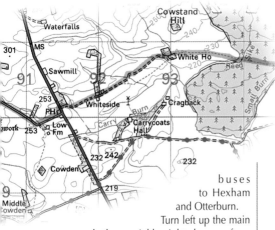

buses
to Hexham
and Otterburn.

Turn left up the main
road, then quickly right down a farm
access road, signposted for North Heugh. Pass a farm at
Whiteside, then continue along the road towards another
farm called **White House**. The right of way veers to the
right, away from the access road, then heads for the farm,
but apart from a gateway in a drystone wall the route isn't
visible on the ground. As a result, walkers may prefer to
stay on the farm access road.

Pass **White House**, then turn left and right through
gates to pass some large outbuildings. ▶

Follow a track onwards and go through two gates to
pass through two large fields. Cross a stile and a small
stream to enter a forest. A path is marked along forest
rides, though it can be wet underfoot, with lots of tussocky grass.

Watch carefully as the route crosses boggy ground
flanking **Small Burn**, then aim for a track and a drystone
wall at the edge of the forest. It is possible to go wrong
on this stretch, being drawn along an easier path leading onto a forest track. If this happens, just continue
onwards to reach the drystone wall at the edge of the
forest.

Turn left to follow the track at the edge of the forest, but leave it as directed by blue bridleway arrows
on marker posts. These show the way to a gate, where a
tussocky, rushy, boggy path leads due north through the

Wade's route ran
from White House
to the Sweethope
Loughs, but this isn't
a right of way, and
the farmer at White
House asks walkers
to stay on the right
of way as described
here.

59

Sweethope Loughs are popular with trout fishermen, but although they lie close to the route, cannot be seen

forest, with views across an unplanted moor later. Pass through two gates well to the right of a cottage.

Cross a footbridge over a stream and set off up a grassy track. Although this track could be followed, a marker post points along a barely trodden path on a tussocky moorland slope, with the route crossing the track on the crest of the moor. Either way, head towards a prominent barn and go through a gate to the right of it. Turn left along a narrow road and drop down from the low rocky brow of **Lunga Crags**.

MYSTERY SHEEPFOLD

What looks like a typical circular drystone Northumberland sheepfold stands beside the road. It is in perfect condition, but contains a mass of boulders that have evidently been blasted from the nearby crag. The sheepfold must have been built around them, since they could never fit through the narrow entrance... but why?

Walk straight ahead by road to reach Cornhills Farmhouse bed and breakfast.

Turn right at a road junction and head down past a cattle-grid, then climb to a road junction. ◄

Turn left and follow another road uphill towards a small forest.

The land between the two roads is access land, and there is a gate at the bottom and top of the moorland slope. Walkers who wish to short-cut may do so, but be warned that the bottom of the slope is boggy and the rest is tussocky and pathless.

Follow the road down around a bend, then turn right as indicated by a bridleway sign at a gate. Follow wheel-marks across the moor, then down to cross **Ray Burn**, before climbing through a stone arch under an **old railway line**. Drift left up a rushy moor, passing close to the rumpled earth and stone remains of an ancient homestead.

Cross pathless heather moor, aiming for a forest fence. Follow the fence over a heathery rise, then go through a gate to follow a path along a forest ride. Join a track and turn right to follow it over a forested crest over 290m (950ft) on **Ray Fell**.

As the track runs downhill it bends to the right, and a marker post points towards very rugged terrain. To be honest, there is no evidence of use, and walkers seem to be voting with their feet, simply following the track all the way down a clear-felled slope. At

map continued on page 62

61

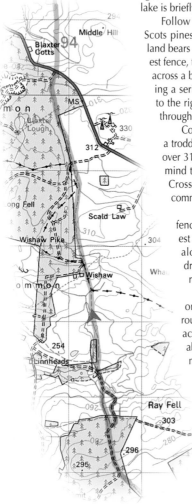

the bottom, do not go through a gate, or follow the track across a stream. Instead, go through a small gate on the right, as marked, and step across the stream. A small lake is briefly in view to the left at **Linnheads**.

Follow a fence uphill beside a plantation of Scots pines. The rugged grass and heather moorland bears some trodden paths, first beside the forest fence, then, after crossing a crest, head straight across a broad and boggy dip in the moors, passing a series of grouse shooting butts. Keep well to the right of two cottages at **Wishaw**, passing through two gates on the way.

Continue up the moorland slope and follow a trodden path alongside another forest. Climb over 310m (1015ft) on **Scald Law**, and bear in mind that some parts may be wet and boggy. Cross over a track and note the prominent communication masts on Mount Gilbert.

Later, go through a gate in the forest fence, but continue to walk beside the forest to reach a corner. Keep straight ahead along a boggy forest ride, which later drops to the junction of a quarry access road and the busy **A696**.

Cross the road and go through a gate onto another moor. The next part of the route isn't a right of way, but it does cross access land that should always be available. Follow a fence that divides heather moorland from grassy moorland, staying on the grassy left-hand side. Go down into a boggy dip, then climb over a crest. Go down to cross a stream then climb to a gate. Go through the gate and head straight for a solitary cottage at **Hillhead**.

There is an intersection of paths and tracks, and the simplest thing to do is keep left of the cottage, then start following a power line

A fence is followed across access land between the busy A696 and a solitary cottage at Hillhead

downhill. During the descent, head well to the right of a shed to cross a farm access road. Cross a ladder-stile and keep left of a low, grassy embankment to continue down through a long field.

Cross stiles at the bottom to reach a road, then turn left to follow the road over a bridge on **Elsdon Burn**. Turn right at a road junction to enter the village of **Elsdon**, where most buildings are arranged around a huge, spacious green.

ELSDON

St Cuthbert's body is said to have rested briefly at Elsdon in 875AD. The current church dates from around 1400, and is known as the 'Mother Church of Redesdale', but there are traces of 11th- or 12th-century work. In 1076 William the Conqueror granted the Lordship of Redesdale to Robert de Umfreville, and a motte and bailey can be distinguished beside the village.

Stout Elsdon Tower has long been associated with the Rectors of St Cuthbert's, and has been recorded since 1415. Various coats-of-arms can be seen around the tower – Umfreville on south wall, Howard on north wall, and Percy above the porch – as patronage changed through the centuries. Elsdon Tower ceased to be church property in 1961 and is now a private residence, but access is permitted just inside the gateway for photographs. It is the best-preserved medieval tower house in the national park, and one of the finest in the Borders. Other interesting features around Elsdon include a pinfold, cockpit and bull-baiting stone.

Elsdon once had four pubs, but now has only The Bird in Bush and a tearoom at the Old School House. Accommodation is limited, and if all beds are taken, then walkers may need to move off-route to Otterburn. Occasional Snaith's buses link Elsdon and Otterburn daily, except Sundays.

OTTERBURN

The Battle of Otterburn took place between English and Scottish forces in 1388. On the Scottish side the Earl of Douglas mounted an attack on Newcastle then suddenly retreated one night. On the English side Harry Hotspur gave chase and covered considerable distance. The English force found the Scottish force at rest in the evening. Hotspur had the advantage of surprise, but didn't wait for his entire force to assemble. As a result neither force was prepared, and they tore at each other through the night. Hotspur was defeated and captured, while Douglas won the day but lost his life. Hundreds of skeletons discovered in a mass grave at Elsdon are believed to be those who were killed at the Battle of Otterburn

Facilities include hotels and a guest house, an ATM and a shop. The Otterburn Mill has a café and visitor centre offering tourist information, tel 01830 520093. Snaith's buses link Otterburn and Newcastle and may divert through Elsdon by request. National Express runs a daily coach service through Otterburn, linking Newcastle and Edinburgh. Munro's of Jedburgh does the same, except Sundays. Arriva buses runs a Sunday service linking Otterburn with Keilder, Newcastle and Hexham.

Elsdon Tower, recorded since 1415, is the best-preserved medieval tower house in the national park

DAY 5

Elsdon to Rothbury via the Moors

Start	Elsdon – NY935932
Finish	Rothbury – NU058017
Distance	22km (13½ miles)
Maps	OS Landrangers 80 and 81 or OS Explorer OL42
Terrain	Open moorlands, pathless in parts, but good paved paths later, giving way to fields and farm roads.
Refreshments	Plenty of choice at Rothbury.
Public Transport	Northumbria buses link Rothbury with Morpeth and Newcastle. Arriva buses operate a limited summer Sunday service.

When Harold Wade wrote his guidebook, he took the route high over the moors from Elsdon to Rothbury, regardless of the absence of rights of way. James Roberts preferred to stay on rights of way, so took his route through extensive forests (see Day 5 Alternative). These days the high moors are designated access land, so most of the time there will be no objection to anyone crossing them, so walk this way and enjoy a high-level moorland traverse.

● Day 5 Alternative

Leave **Elsdon** via the road signposted for Rothbury, but only to cross a bridge. Turn right along a narrow farm road signposted for **Whiskershiel**. The road runs

map continued on page 68

through wide-open fields, reaching a junction. Keep straight ahead and pass two farms at **Landshot**, then turn left to cross a ladder-stile.

Drop down into a dip to cross a footbridge, then turn left to climb alongside a drystone wall. The easiest walking is some distance to the left of the wall. Pass through a gateway at a junction of walls. Climb higher to the junction of a wall and fence, then turn right to cross a stile beside a gate on **Landshot Hill**.

Follow the drystone wall across a grassy moorland slope to reach a forest. At this point the right of way enters

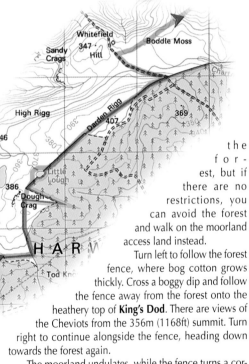

the forest, but if there are no restrictions, you can avoid the forest and walk on the moorland access land instead.

Turn left to follow the forest fence, where bog cotton grows thickly. Cross a boggy dip and follow the fence away from the forest onto the heathery top of **King's Dod**. There are views of the Cheviots from the 356m (1168ft) summit. Turn right to continue alongside the fence, heading down towards the forest again.

The moorland undulates, while the fence turns a corner. Climb again onto **Dough Crag**, away from the forest,

View of the Cheviot Hills and Caiston Lake from the rugged moorland edge of Tosson Hill

to reach a gate and a junction of fences on the 385m (1263ft) summit. The fence to the left leads off-route down to Darden Lough, while the fence to the right leads to Little Lough.

Keep right for the Reivers Way, but keep to the left side of **Little Lough**, on level, boggy ground. Climb again beside the forest fence and follow it past a shelter cairn. This sits on the heathery crest of **Darden Rigg** at 406m (1332ft).

The fence later drops downhill to reach a gate. Don't go

through it, but turn left, away from the forest, down a clear moorland track. After the interlude walking on access land, the route is now on a right of way again.

Cross **Boddle Moss**, then, when a line of corrugated-iron grouse butts are reached, look right to spot a broad path mown straight through the heather. This path was confirmed as a right of way in April 2005. ▸

Anyone looking for a short-cut avoiding Rothbury could continue down the track to Hepple.

Follow the path across a broad dip, then climb over a heathery hump to cross a lesser dip. Beyond this, the path climbs onto a gritstone crag on **Tosson Hill**, where a cairn shelter encloses a trig point at 440m (1444ft). This is a splendid viewpoint, embracing the Cheviots, Northumberland coast and north Pennines.

A narrow but fairly clear path runs along the heathery crest, passing occasional marker posts on the way to a forest at **Ravens Heugh**. Cross a step-stile and follow a well-worn path through a heathery swathe in the forest. A track leads to a junction with another track, where a left turn leads to a noticeboard.

map continued from page 66

● Day 5 Alternative

69

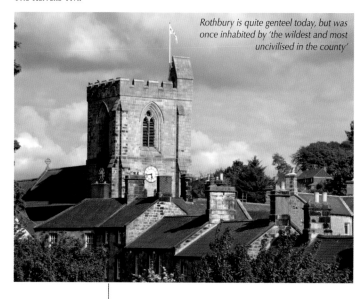

Rothbury is quite genteel today, but was once inhabited by 'the wildest and most uncivilised in the county'

Neither Wade nor Roberts made the best use of the Simonside Hills. Both of them descended too early into forest, and Wade included too much road-walking to Rothbury.

Climb straight up a steep and bouldery path, flanked by heather and bilberry. A stone-slab path leads along a prominent gritstone edge to a cairn on top of **Simonside** at 429m (1407ft). This is a splendid viewpoint for Coquetdale, with the Cheviot Hills rising to the north. ◀

There are two ways to continue – via either a clear, stone-slab path along the crest of the Simonside Hills to **Dove Crag**, or a more rugged path traversing at a slightly lower level. Either way, descend from the large cairn on Dove Crag later and cross a ladder-stile over a fence. A clear path romps over a couple of heathery humps then drops downhill. Stone steps lead to a road and a car park.

A clear path climbs from the car park, signposted for Rothbury and marked by posts. Watch for a rock and a metal sign off to the left, where ancient 'cup-and-ring' marks can be inspected. There are other examples on the hill, but this is the easiest to spot from the path. Follow the path over the hillside and down into a valley, drifting right at the bottom. Pass a small pond and climb to a stone house at **Whittondean**.

Turn left to follow an access track away from the house, then right downhill from a junction. The track later passes a stone tower. This is Sharp's Folly, built in the mid-18th century. It is the oldest folly in Northumberland, and was constructed to give relief to unemployed stonemasons.

Keep left to join a minor road in the village of **Whitton**, then turn left again down the road to the fine old house of Whitton Tower. Turn right at a road junction – not down the road to Rothbury, but along a field path instead. This quickly links with a road leading down to a four-arched bridge spanning the River Coquet. Simply cross the bridge and walk into the centre of **Rothbury**. Most of the town's facilities are found by turning left, which is the way the route goes.

ROTHBURY

Bronze Age and Iron Age settlements and ritual sites abound around Rothbury, while the Simonside Hills are crowned with prominent burial cairns, with intriguing 'cup-and-ring'-marked stones on their flanks. The village of Rothbury probably dates from the seventh century, and a fragment of a Saxon cross in All Saints church may date from around 800AD. Reliable historical records start in 1125, and the area suffered as much as any other during centuries of border strife. The *Guide to Northumberland* of 1888 noted, 'The people of Rothbury...were among the wildest and most uncivilised in the county. For fighting, gaming and drinking they had a worse reputation than the inhabitants of Tynedale or Redesdale.' Nowadays the village has a genteel air about it, and the central parts feature several splendid, solid, stone buildings.

Rothbury has a full range of services, easily the greatest so far along the Reivers Way. There are two banks, one with an ATM, a post office, several shops, pubs and restaurants, plus a range of accommodation. Although there is a Railway

Hotel, there is no longer a railway line. There is a joint Northumberland national park and tourist information centre, tel 01669 620887. Northumbria buses run daily, linking Rothbury with Morpeth and Newcastle. Arriva buses runs a limited service on summer Sundays.

CRAGSIDE HOUSE AND COUNTRY PARK

Cragside is well named, being perched on a crag outside Rothbury. It was the home of the Victorian inventor and engineer Lord Armstrong, and is surrounded by a huge rock garden and extensive woodlands, managed by the National Trust, with a restaurant on site. If making a visit, it is probably best to reserve most of a day for it. Cragside was the first house in the world to be lit by hydroelectric power, and examples of Armstrong's engineering triumphs can be seen in the Power House. The estate is open from mid-morning, while the house is open in the afternoons from mid-March to early November. It is usually closed on Mondays, but open on bank holiday Mondays. There is an entry charge, tel 01669 620333, www.nationaltrust.org.uk.

DAY 5 ALTERNATIVE
Elsdon to Rothbury via the Forests

Start	Elsdon – NY935932
Finish	Rothbury – NU058017
Distance	21km (13 miles)
Maps	OS Landrangers 80 and 81 or OS Explorer OL42
Terrain	Extensive forest, with some difficult paths and easy tracks. Heather moorland, with some rugged paths and some easy paths.
Refreshments	Plenty of choice at Rothbury.
Public Transport	Northumbria buses link Rothbury with Morpeth and Newcastle. Arriva buses operates a limited summer Sunday service.

Harold Wade's original route between Elsdon and Rothbury is the main Day 5 route in this guide, but if the high moors, which are designated access land, are closed for grouse shooting or other activities, this alternative, largely forested route on rights of way, remains available. It was described by James Roberts in the original Cicerone guidebook to the Reviers Way, but now serves best as an alternative. It is not as scenic as the moorland route, and some paths can be awkward.

Leave **Elsdon** via the road signposted for Rothbury, but only to cross a bridge. Turn right along a narrow farm road signposted for **Whiskershiel**. The road runs through wide-open fields, reaching a junction. Keep right to pass two farms at **Landshot** and head downhill a little.

Turn right across a bridge before Whiskershiel and follow the road uphill into a forest. Stay on the tarmac to reach a house at **Whitlees**. The low stone ruins of a 'bastle', or fortified farmhouse, can be seen in the back garden.

Turn right up a forest path signposted for Manside Cross. The path follows a grassy ride up to a junction of forest tracks. Go straight ahead, but quickly branch left as marked along a heathery ride. Drainage ditches along the way are equipped with little footbridges or steps. Cross a forest track and continue

Leaving Elsdon along the alternative route on a frosty winter morning, hoping wet ground later will be frozen!

as marked.
When a junction of forest tracks is reached, again continue as marked, enjoying views across a clear-felled area.

An open space is reached at **Manside Cross**, at 325m (1066ft). All that remains of an old stone cross is set into a socket in a square base. It stands beside the corner of a fence where a stile should be crossed. There is also a prominent earth-

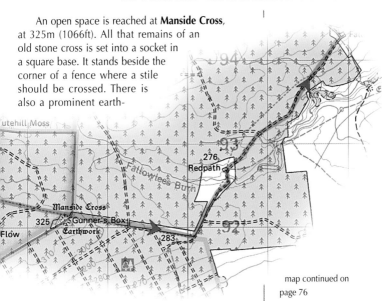

map continued on page 76

work nearby, the remains of an ancient settlement. There is a view to the Simonside Hills.

Looking roughly east, a broad swathe of moorland has been left unplanted between two extensive parts of **Harwood Forest**. There is plenty of tussocky grass, and while the right of way hugs the forest fence, most walkers will be happy to wander along wheel-marks left by occasional vehicle traffic. The wheel-marks lead to a gate and a firm track, while the fence and right of way leads to a stile and footbridge to reach the track.

Another dilemma has to be faced on a corner of the track, where there is a gate. The right of way goes through the gate to continue along another rough and tussocky unplanted swathe, but there is no trodden path, and an awkward barbed-wire fence lies halfway to the next firm track. A good work-around from the corner is simply to follow the track, which runs parallel to the fence anyway, and is marked as the Border County Ride. When the track

map continued from page 75

See map on page 69 for remainder of route.

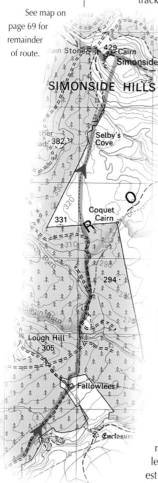

bends right, keep straight ahead alongside the fence, where the ground alongside bears some kind of trodden path, though it is boggy in places. When the next firm track is reached, turn left to follow it.

The track leaves the forest for a while, and enters a large area of unplanted moorland around the isolated farmstead of **Redpath**, with the Simonside Hills seen far beyond. Footpath and bridleway markers point either side of the track, but it is best to stay on the track as it runs back into the forest. Keep following it straight ahead until another isolated farmstead is reached at **Fallowlees**. There is a fine, forest-free view southwards here.

Turn left along a track to leave Fallowlees, then right as indicated by a bridleway marker, to walk alongside a drystone wall behind the farm. Veer left away from the wall to cross a clear-felled area, then cross a forest track. If this stretch looks too difficult to walk, because of clear-felling, then simply follow the track away from Fallowlees, turning right at a cross-tracks, to reach the point where the bridleway crosses.

Walk down a roughly vegetated forest ride from one track to another, then turn left to cross a bridge over **Newbiggin Burn**. Follow the track uphill and stay on it, heading roughly northwards from clear-felled to standing forest. When the track suddenly makes a pronounced bend to the left, leave it to walk straight ahead along a forest ride, as marked. Cross over a stile at the edge of the forest.

A rocky cleft is passed at Selby's Cove as the alternative route approaches the Simonside Hills

A clear, but often boggy and overtrodden path runs across a broad dip on extensive heather moorland. A couple of stretches feature board-walks. Climb beside a forest fence, where there is a view of a fine little crag face in **Selby's Cove**.

Cross a stile and walk down a rugged slope. This was once forested, then clear-felled, and has since reverted to moorland. The path is very fiddly, so watch for a series of marker posts. These show the way through a corner of a forest, then there is a gradual ascent through another clear-felled area, eventually reaching a track and a noticeboard.

Climb straight up a steep and bouldery path, flanked by heather and bilberry. A stone-slab path leads along a prominent gritstone edge to a cairn on top of **Simonside** at 429m (1407ft). This is a splendid viewpoint for Coquetdale, with the Cheviot Hills rising to the north. (Neither Wade nor Roberts made the best use of the Simonside Hills. Both of them descended too early into forest, and Wade included too much road-walking to Rothbury.)

The view from a rocky outcrop on the heathery Simonside Hills, looking towards Dove Crag

There are two ways to continue – either along a clear stone-slab path along the crest of the Simonside Hills to **Dove Crag**, or along a more rugged path traversing at a slightly lower level. Either way, descend from the large cairn on Dove Crag later and cross a ladder-stile over a fence. A clear path romps over a couple of heathery humps then drops downhill. Stone steps lead to a road and a car park.

A clear path climbs from the car park, signposted for Rothbury and marked by posts. Watch for a rock and a metal sign off to the left, where ancient 'cup-and-ring' marks can be inspected. There are other examples on the hill, but this is the easiest to spot from the path. Follow the path over the hillside and down into a valley, drifting right at the bottom. Pass a small pond and climb to a stone house at **Whittondean**.

Turn left to follow an access track away from the house, then right downhill from a junction. The track later passes a stone tower. This is Sharp's Folly, built in the mid-18th century. It is the oldest folly in Northumberland, and was constructed to give relief to unemployed stonemasons.

Keep left to join a minor road in the village of **Whitton**, then turn left again down the road to the fine old house of Whitton Tower. Turn right at a road junction – not down the road to Rothbury, but along a field path instead. This quickly links with a road leading down to a four-arched bridge spanning the River Coquet. Simply cross the bridge and walk into the centre of **Rothbury** (see end of Day 5 main route, page 71, for details).

DAY 6

Rothbury to Uswayford

Start	Rothbury – NU058017
Finish	Uswayford – NT887145
Distance	32km (20 miles)
Maps	OS Landrangers 80 and 81 or OS Explorers 332 and OL16
Terrain	Easy, low-level paths, tracks and roads, mostly among fields. Exposed moorland tracks and forest tracks later.
Refreshments	Thropton, Harbottle and Alwinton all have pubs. Evening meals are available at Uswayford only if arranged in advance.
Public Transport	A 'post bus' service operates from Morpeth to Rothbury, then links Holystone, Harbottle and Alwinton. It runs twice each way, Monday to Friday, and once each way on Saturdays.

When Harold Wade walked the Reivers Way in 1975, he was unimpressed with the gravel pits beside the River Coquet, while in 1992 James Roberts charted a wide detour from the river in the original Cicerone guide. The gravel pits have since been landscaped and are popular with bird-watchers. Little villages give way to a delightful walk along the high-level moorland track of Clennel Street. This is a long day's walk and you need to be sure of a bed and a meal at the end of it.

Leave **Rothbury** by walking along Front Street in the direction of Thropton. There are actually two parallel streets and they join at Rothbury House. Turn right up a minor road, keeping straight ahead at a junction as signposted for Pondicherry.

The road splits at the bottom, so keep straight ahead, or right, and climb to pass through a gate for West Hills Farm. As the road bends left towards the farm, keep straight ahead as marked to follow a path uphill beside a drystone wall.

Little osson

Cross a step-stile near a 3500-year-old burial mound, then over rough pasture, and look downhill to spot the circular embankment of a 2300-year-old **hill fort**. The enclosure contains hut circles. Cross a stile over a wall, walk down a field and cross a stile over another wall.

Continue down through another field and cross a stile onto Physic Lane. Turn left down the lane to reach the Cross Keys pub on the **B6341**. Turn right to walk across a bridge into the village of **Thropton**.

THROPTON

Facilities include the Three Wheat Heads Inn, accommodation, post office shop, a daily bus service linking with Rothbury and Morpeth, and a 'post bus' service linking villages through the Coquet valley.

After crossing the bridge, either turn left and follow a riverside path skirting **Thropton**, or follow the road through the village and turn left at the village hall to reach the river. Both routes reach a footbridge spanning the **River Coquet**.

Cross the bridge and turn right, passing through a gate while heading upstream. The path pulls away from the river and heads through level fields towards some

map continued on page 84

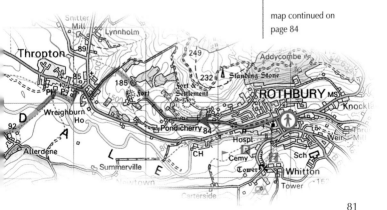

Looking across the River Coquet near Thropton towards the heathery humps of the Simonside Hills

farm buildings. Go through a gate and cross a track, then keep well to the right of the buildings at **Ryehill** to go through another gate onto a track.

Turn right along the track and pass a gateway, then turn left to walk beside a field as signposted for Bickerton. After passing through another gate, head for some distant cattle troughs to find yet another gate. Pass between trees and follow a track beside an old gravel pit, now a lake with islands for wildfowl. The track becomes uncomfortably cobbly underfoot, but after turning a couple of corners, a small gate allows access to a field where walkers can continue parallel to the track.

If walking in the field, turn left through another gate to reach a junction of tracks in a wooded area, but if following the track anyway, turn left at the junction. There are embankments beside the track, which becomes narrower and grassier, as well as a series of bird-hides allowing views over **Caistron Lake**. ▶

After going through a gate towards the head of the lake, cross a stile beside a gate on the left then cross a field diagonally. Although it is difficult to see ahead to **Bickerton**, keep left of the buildings to reach a minor road. Turn right up the road, then head gently downhill past the forest at **Newton Park**, passing the access road for **Hepple Whitefield**.

The road overlooks a huge meander on the River Coquet, then a path can be used to short-cut across a corner of a field to reach a bridge over the river. The road runs up to the tiny village of **Hepple**, which has a 'post bus' service. Either climb all the way up to a road junction, or short-cut left up a signposted field path.

Turn left at the signposted road junction and follow a narrow road to its very end at **West Hepple**. Turn left along a track above the last buildings, then turn right up a grassy track. Turn left and right beside a small forest plantation, then follow blue bridleway arrows, lining up a series of gates while dropping gently through fields between other small forest plantations.

When a broad riverside meadow is reached, turn right and follow a vague way made by farm vehicles,

Look out for swans, mallards, geese, coot, moorhen, tufted duck, pochard, goldeneye, little and great crested grebes, cormorants, gadwall, garden warbler, sand martins, house martins and swallows. Otters may be spotted too.

map continued on
page 86

which avoids thistles and molehills alongside. Stones can be used to cross a muddy ditch, then a gate gives access to a footbridge over the **River Coquet**. A road lies just beyond and a left turn leads to the lovely little village of **Holystone**.

HOLYSTONE

Holystone's name is supposedly derived from a 'holy stone' at the

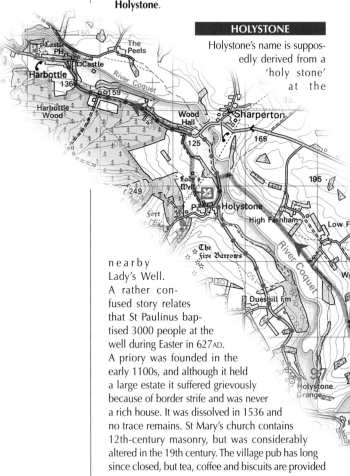

nearby Lady's Well. A rather confused story relates that St Paulinus baptised 3000 people at the well during Easter in 627AD. A priory was founded in the early 1100s, and although it held a large estate it suffered grievously because of border strife and was never a rich house. It was dissolved in 1536 and no trace remains. St Mary's church contains 12th-century masonry, but was considerably altered in the 19th century. The village pub has long since closed, but tea, coffee and biscuits are provided on a help-yourself basis in the church. A 'post bus' service links with nearby villages and Rothbury.

Leave the village by following a track to **Lady's Well**, to find a spring-fed pool in a wooded enclosure, with a stone cross in the water. Follow a waymarked path beyond the well, using gates and stiles to pass through fields where alpacas may be grazing, and follow a track to a road at **Wood Hall**. Turn left to follow the road gently uphill and downhill to reach the village of **Harbottle**.

HARBOTTLE

There are two Harbottle castles, one either side of the village. The 'big house' of Harbottle Castle is the most obvious, while the ruins of an older Harbottle Castle are barely noticed on top of a grassy hill. The old castle was once of great importance, having been a baronial seat, royal castle and administrative centre for the Lordship of Redesdale. Facilities in the village are limited. The Star Inn has a very basic shop attached. Accommodation is available at the Byre. There is a 'post bus' service back to Rothbury and onwards to Alwinton.

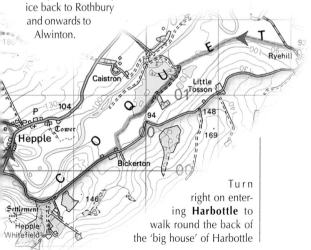

Turn right on entering **Harbottle** to walk round the back of the 'big house' of Harbottle

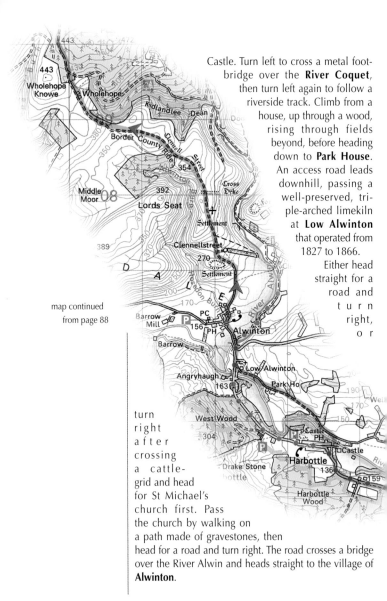

Castle. Turn left to cross a metal foot-bridge over the **River Coquet**, then turn left again to follow a riverside track. Climb from a house, up through a wood, rising through fields beyond, before heading down to **Park House**. An access road leads downhill, passing a well-preserved, tri-ple-arched limekiln at **Low Alwinton** that operated from 1827 to 1866.

Either head straight for a road and turn right, or

map continued from page 88

turn right after crossing a cattle-grid and head for St Michael's church first. Pass the church by walking on a path made of gravestones, then head for a road and turn right. The road crosses a bridge over the River Alwin and heads straight to the village of **Alwinton**.

ALWINTON

This little village offers only limited facilities, but more importantly, the last real opportunity to obtain anything before Wooler. If arriving late in the day, re-assess your chances of reaching Uswayford, or play safe and stop in the village for the night. Accommodation is available, either in the village or at nearby Clennell Hall Hotel, which also includes a campsite and shop. There is a pub and tea room in the village and a 'post bus' service back to Rothbury.

Turn right to leave the village for **Clennell Street** as signposted. A narrow tarmac road soon gives way to a broad and stony track climbing towards the Cheviot Hills. Pass through a gate and keep well to the left of a small farm. There are no gates for a while, so simply climb and keep left of a fence, noting that there are ancient earthworks straddling the crest of the hill. These include a hill fort, settlement sites and the defensive **Cross Dyke**.

One stretch of the track is like a rollercoaster, later running down through a gate. Cross a dip, that might

The old highway of Clennell Street is a fine gravel track as it climbs into the Cheviot Hills from Alwinton

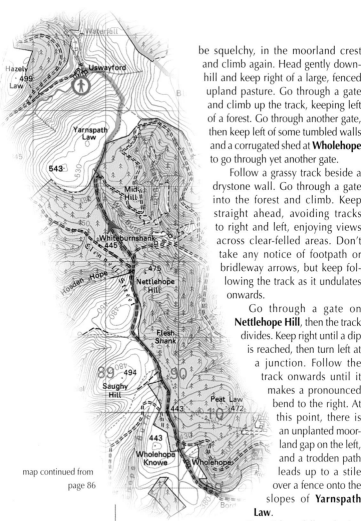

be squelchy, in the moorland crest and climb again. Head gently downhill and keep right of a large, fenced upland pasture. Go through a gate and climb up the track, keeping left of a forest. Go through another gate, then keep left of some tumbled walls and a corrugated shed at **Wholehope** to go through yet another gate.

Follow a grassy track beside a drystone wall. Go through a gate into the forest and climb. Keep straight ahead, avoiding tracks to right and left, enjoying views across clear-felled areas. Don't take any notice of footpath or bridleway arrows, but keep following the track as it undulates onwards.

Go through a gate on **Nettlehope Hill**, then the track divides. Keep right until a dip is reached, then turn left at a junction. Follow the track onwards until it makes a pronounced bend to the right. At this point, there is an unplanted moorland gap on the left, and a trodden path leads up to a stile over a fence onto the slopes of **Yarnspath Law**.

map continued from page 86

Turn right to follow the forest fence, though keep away from a boggy patch alongside it for a while. Follow the path as it drifts left, away from the forest, to cross a moorland gap over 500m (1640ft). There is a stile over a fence, but the trodden way

goes through a nearby gate. A squelchy path leads down a moorland slope, eventually reaching the remote farm of **Uswayford**.

Walkers cross a moorland gap on Yarnspath Law before descending to the remote farmstead of Uswayford

USWAYFORD

The remote farmhouse at Uswayford, pronounced 'Yoosy-ford', is the only place offering dinner, bed and breakfast in the heart of the Cheviot Hills. If planning to stay here, check availability well in advance, and if necessary structure your entire walk to take advantage of a spare bed! The farm has long provided accommodation, but cannot cope with walkers turning up unannounced. If the farmhouse is fully booked, a basic bunkhouse and camping is available 6km (3¾ miles) down-dale at Barrowburn. If using the bunkhouse you will need your own food supplies and a sleeping bag.

DAY 7

Uswayford to Wooler via the Cheviot

Start	Uswayford – NT887145
Finish	Wooler – NT994283
Distance	24km (15 miles)
Maps	OS Landrangers 75 and 80 or OS Explorer OL16
Terrain	A forested ascent gives way to clear hill paths, followed by paths and tracks from valley to valley.
Refreshments	Plenty of choice at Wooler.
Public Transport	Regular daily Glen Valley buses link Wooler with Berwick-upon-Tweed. Travelsure buses link Wooler with Chillingham, Chatton and Alnwick.

When Harold Wade walked the Reivers Way he crossed the Cheviot, but James Roberts was concerned that the descent via Scald Hill wasn't a right of way. In fact, it was always a popular route, and finally designated as a right of way in January 2008. The broad, bleak and boggy Cheviot is the highest point in Northumberland, and in fine weather should be regarded as the crowning glory of the Reivers Way. In this guide it is described first, but the low-level alternative, via Linhope, is also included – see Day 7 Alternative. The final part of this day's walk links with St Cuthbert's Way.

Just above the farmyard at **Uswayford**, a small gate overlooks Usway Burn and a path leads down to a **footbridge**. Cross over and head upstream, climbing from the flow towards a corner of a forest. ◄

It is possible to detour 10 minutes upstream to see a waterfall at Davidson's Linn.

Turn left uphill, and a clear path soon climbs straight up through the forest, crossing a track at a higher level, reaching open, grassy moorland at a gate and stile.

Walk to a signpost and turn right along a grassy track that rises gently to another gate and stile. Continue over heather moorland to reach the course of the **Pennine**

Way, at 542m (1778ft), which follows a fence along the English and Scottish border.

Turn right to follow an obvious, stone-slabbed path beside the border fence. This moorland was once badly over-trodden, and all who recall those days will be grateful for the stone path.

It leads via **Butt Roads** to a junction of fences on a gentle saddle. After a short break, the stone slabs resume and lead past a lone trig

THE CHEVIOT

map continued on page 93

point at 531m (1742ft) at **King's Seat**.

A gradual ascent passes **Score Head**, then there is a steeper climb on a peaty moorland slope. ▶

As the path levels out, a boardwalk leads to a junction of fences.

The Pennine Way turns left along a wooden boardwalk for **Auchope Cairn**, while the Reivers Way and an optional spur of the Pennine Way run

Growing among the heather, bilberry and bog cotton are abundant cloudberries – an arctic remnant plant producing white flowers in spring and orange berries in summer.

● Day 7 Alternative

91

The stoutly buttressed trig point at 815m (2674ft) on The Cheviot – the highest point on the Reivers Way

straight ahead along a stone-slab path towards **Cairn Hill**. The slabs run out on the gentle ascent, while the path passes a fence junction, shelter cairn and signpost on the 776m (2546ft) summit. The soft, grass-covered peat can be squelchy when wet, but there are more stone slabs again while crossing a broad saddle on boggier heather moorland.

Climb gently and cross step-stiles over two fences to reach the summit of **The Cheviot** at 815m (2674ft). The trig point was constructed at ground level, but over the years a vast thickness of peat has been washed from the summit, requiring the structure to be buttressed with concrete to prevent its collapse. The summit area is broad, bleak and boggy, and despite its height is not a particularly good viewpoint.

DANIEL DEFOE ON THE CHEVIOT

Daniel Defoe travelled extensively around Britain, and was a little too enthusiastic when he compared British scenes with landscapes he had seen elsewhere in the world. The Cheviot was not immune from 'over-interpretation' in 1726, when he compared it to El Teide on Tenerife, or imagined during the ascent that the summit would turn out to be a pinnacle!

'We were the more uneasy about, mounting highery because we all had a Notion, that when we came to the Top, we should be just as upon a Pinnacle, that the Hill narrowed to a Point, and we should have only Room enough to stand, with a Precipice every way round us; and with these Apprehensions, we all sat down upon the Ground, and said we would go no farther. Our Guide did not at first understand what we were apprehensive of; but at last by our Discourse he perceived the Mistake, and then not mocking our Fears, he told us, that indeed if it had been so, we had been in the Right, but he assur'd us, there was Room enough on the Top of the Hill to run a Race, if we thought fit, and we need not fear any thing of being blown off the Precipice, as we had suggested; so he Encouraging us we went on, and reach't the Top of the Hill in about half an Hour more.'

Follow the stone-slab path onwards beside a fence, then cross a ladder-stile beside a gate. The slabs end, but the path is well-trodden and begins to descend steeply parallel to the

● Day 7 Alternative

Broadstruther

383

Broadhope Hill 517

Blacksea Hill

Scald Hill 549

THE CHEVIOT
815

map continued on page 94

93

fence. The vegetation on the slope is short, and there are occasional rashes of scree.

Simply follow the fence downhill, turning left round a corner and crossing a broad, peaty saddle. Climb past a junction of fences, crossing a step-stile to reach the gentle top of **Scald Hill** at 548m (1798ft).

The fence guides you onwards downhill and turns

map continued from page 93

left at a corner. Cross another broad, peaty saddle and climb onto the shoulder of **Broadhope Hill** to reach a gate at a corner. Go through the gate and walk straight ahead along a vague and rugged moorland path. ◄

Descend gradually to a junction with another path and continue towards a solitary cottage flanked by a few trees at **Broadstruther**. (The Day 7 Alternative route joins at this point.) Pass in front of the cottage and follow a track downhill, but watch for a path heading left down to a **footbridge**.

Note the curious geometric patterns created by selectively burning swathes of heather on the surrounding moors.

Climb from the bridge to pass a stile by a gate, then continue straight ahead across a rugged slope well above the river. Go through a gate into what the map shows as forest, but which is mostly bracken and broom. Head downhill and cross a footbridge over **Carey Burn**, then turn right to walk downstream. A marker post shows where the path later climbs from the river, as a delightful green ribbon on an otherwise

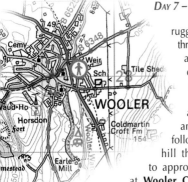

rugged slope. Go through a gate and a gentler ascent continues over moorland.

Turn right along a broad and stony track, following it downhill through a gate to approach buildings at **Wooler Common**. Turn left and right to pass the buildings as signposted, then later turn left down a grassy path to reach a marker post for St Cuthbert's Way. Head up to a small gate and go into a forest to follow a grassy path straight uphill.

Veer slightly right to head downhill, and later go through a gate to leave the forest. A grassy path leads downhill and a gate leads to **Waud House**. Turn left down the access road, then turn right along another road and follow it into the centre of **Wooler**.

WOOLER

Wooler's name has nothing to do with wool, but because of its location in an area heavily grazed by sheep, it has been a notable centre for the wool trade. The Barony of Wooler was created in 1107, and although there was only a tiny settlement in the area, in 1199 it was granted a charter to hold markets and fairs. There seems to have been a castle in the 13th century, rebuilt in the 16th century, but very little remains of it today. Despite being in 'reiver country', Wooler has enjoyed many periods of prosperity, and was always associated with the Earls of Tankerville, who lived at Chillingham Castle.

Wooler has a fine range of facilities, including hotels and other lodgings, banks and a post office, all with ATMs, a range of shops, pubs and restaurants. Glen Valley buses operate from a small

The parish church at Wooler

bus station, linking Wooler with Berwick-upon-Tweed, while Travelsure buses run to Alnwick. Tourist information is available at the Cheviot Centre, tel 01668 282123.

DAY 7 ALTERNATIVE
Uswayford to Wooler via Linhope

Start	Uswayford – NT887145
Finish	Wooler – NT994283
Distance	29km (18 miles)
Maps	OS Landrangers 75, 80 and 81 or OS Explorer OL16
Terrain	Mostly rugged moorland paths and tracks, sometimes wet and boggy, or vague and ill-defined. Some parts run through forests.
Refreshments	Plenty of choice at Wooler.
Public Transport	Regular daily Glen Valley buses link Wooler with Berwick-upon-Tweed. Travelsure buses link Wooler with Chillingham, Chatton and Alnwick.

This route runs at a lower level than the route across the Cheviot, but bear in mind that it is longer, and rather fiddly in terms of route-finding. If foul weather rules out an ascent of the Cheviot, then this route might at least be free of mist and strong winds. It also crosses a couple of roads, offering opportunities to be picked up by car if you are covering the route in short and easy stages. The final part of this day's walk links with St Cuthbert's Way.

Just above the farmyard at **Uswayford**, a small gate over-looks Usway Burn and a path leads down to a footbridge. Don't cross the bridge, but cross a stile and follow a narrow path upstream on a steep and grassy slope.

Ford **Clay Burn** and head upstream. There is no trodden path, so it is worth climbing a little uphill to a forest, then turning right to follow a path beside the forest fence. Later, drop down to cross a stile over a fence and continue upstream.

The valley bottom hasn't been planted with trees and is covered in tussocky grass. A marker post is reached, bearing a blue bridleway arrow, pointing across a small stream. It indicates a path running up a grassy forest ride, and this is the **Salter's Road**. ▶

As the name Salter's Road suggests, pack-horses laden with salt were once driven along it, though in the 13th century it was called the Thieves Road.

When a forest track is reached, turn right along it, but soon turn left to continue across boggy moorland. Wheel-marks lead to a gate on a broad gap, where a morass lies on the other side.

map continued on page 101

Keep to the most obvious track across the moors, then descend to reach a fence. Technically, the bridleway goes through a gate but later swings right and runs downhill beside the fence. Most walkers don't go through the gate, but simply follow the fence straight downhill, crossing a grassy hump at **Nagshead Knowe** before dropping down to a shed and a sheepfold. There is a good view up the valley to the Cheviot. Keep following the track, crossing a stream then later passing a gate to cross a footbridge over the **River Breamish**.

The ascent of High Cantle could be awkward. A bridleway starts from a gate at a nearby railway carriage shed. It runs up a slope of bracken to reach a small gate in a fence, but is difficult when the bracken is high. Beyond that point, a couple of marker posts indicate a faint path climbing higher, crossing over a track, heading for the higher moors to reach another small gate in a fence near the top of **High Cantle**.

If this route looks difficult, then try an alternative approach. Turn left up a clear track before reaching the gate and railway carriage shelter. Turn right through a gate in a fence, then follow wheel-marks up a grassy slope. Turn left along another track, which itself bends right to

head for the top of **High Cantle**. Head left, as marked, to reach the same small gate in the fence that the bridleway leads to.

Go through the gate from tussocky grass to heather moorland. Follow the path as marked, and go through another small gate in a fence, close to the 482m (1581ft) summit of **High Cantle**. Follow a faint path away from the fence, across the moors, gently downhill to reach a broader set of wheel-marks.

A cairn on the moorland crest between High Cantle and Ritto Hill, where a grassy track offers easy walking

Turn left to follow this track across the boggy moors, rising to pass a bouldery cairn. Keep following the track, no matter how much it twists and turns, and later go through a gate to approach rounded **Ritto Hill**.

Drift left from the hill, and on the way downhill go through another gate to reach a forest. At this point, although the Reivers Way turns right to follow the forest fence, it is worth turning left to follow a signposted path to the nearby waterfall of **Linhope Spout**. ◄

A visit to Linhope Spout adds half an hour to the day's walk

The forest fence is accompanied by a broad track that leads down into the tiny estate village of **Linhope**, where a road crosses Linhope Burn.

Follow the narrow road uphill, passing a forest entrance, then turning left up a stony track signposted as a bridleway. Go through gates, then cross a field below an **ancient settlement** site. Go through another gate, then down a little to ford a stream. Rise gently, and to avoid confusion between several paths, aim to keep well to the right of a railway carriage shed, to go through another gate.

The grassy track splits, so keep right, heading roughly northeast, climbing gently to reach a wall in the distance. Go through a gate, then keep left of a black shed ahead. Follow the grassy track across grass and bracken moorland, passing a marker post and later going straight through an intersection of paths. The track swings left after **Cunyan Crags** and climbs, reaching a stile and gate at a junction of fences at a forest corner.

The next part can be tricky. Cross the stile and keep right to follow the forest fence. This is awkward because the branches push walkers too close to the fence. Later, a marker post directs walkers into the dark forest, where the ground is soft and muddy, before linking with a grassy track. When this grassy track is followed, another marker post directs walkers to the right, back among the trees, then, after re-joining the track later, a post directs walkers to the left, again into the trees, before the route crosses another forest track.

Alternatively, instead of trying to follow the marked footpath, start by following the forest fence. Don't follow the fence on the same side as the forest, however, but on the open moorland instead, which is access land. A joining fence needs to be crossed, then later turn left through a small gate into the forest. Quickly turn right onto the grassy forest track, but stay on it for easier walking. The track leads gently downhill, uphill, then downhill again. Turn left along another forest track, until a marker post is seen on the right.

Whichever route is chosen, take the path down a forest ride as marked. The ground is boggy, then becomes badly over-trodden where a small footbridge is crossed. Take care to spot the correct line straight through a dark part of the forest, confirmed later by marker posts, to reach the edge of the forest at a stile and small gate. Turn right to reach a footbridge near remote **Threestoneburn House**.

Don't cross the footbridge, but head upstream, with a view of Hedgehope Hill at the head of the valley. Cross a stile by a small gate, cross two small footbridges over **Threestone Burn**, then cross another stile by a small gate to enter a forest. Note a small **stone circle** off to the left. Walk up a forest track to reach a stile by a gate at the edge of the forest.

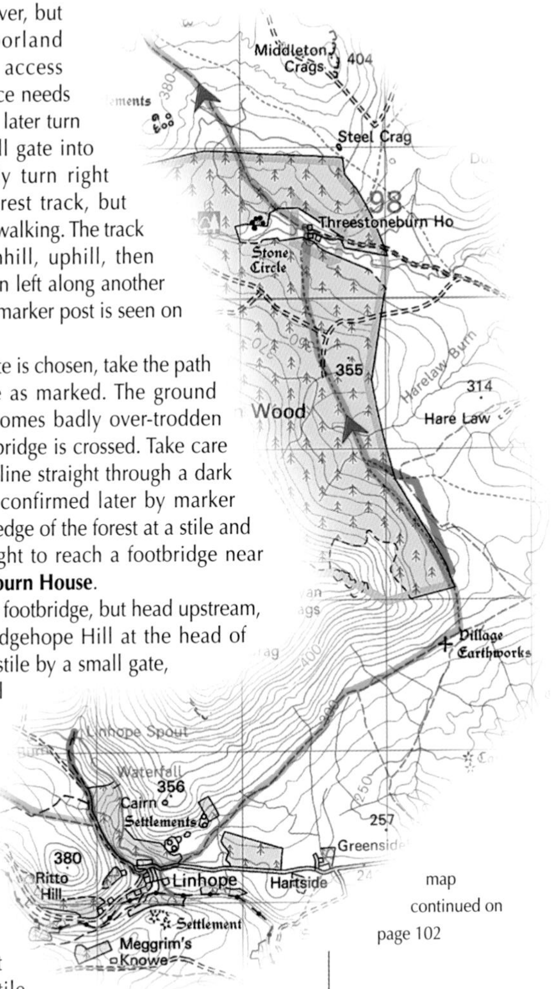

map continued on page 102

101

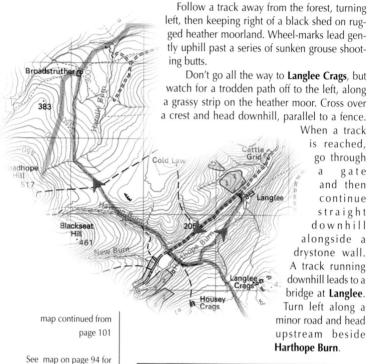

Follow a track away from the forest, turning left, then keeping right of a black shed on rugged heather moorland. Wheel-marks lead gently uphill past a series of sunken grouse shooting butts.

Don't go all the way to **Langlee Crags**, but watch for a trodden path off to the left, along a grassy strip on the heather moor. Cross over a crest and head downhill, parallel to a fence. When a track is reached, go through a gate and then continue straight downhill alongside a drystone wall. A track running downhill leads to a bridge at **Langlee**. Turn left along a minor road and head upstream beside **Harthope Burn**.

map continued from page 101

See map on page 94 for remainder of route.

LANGLEEFORD

As a young man, Walter Scott visited the Cheviot Hills with his uncle in 1791. Failing to find lodgings in Wooler, they stayed at Langleeford. Scott wrote to a friend: 'All the day we shoot, fish, walk and ride; dine and sup upon fish struggling from the stream, and the most delicious heath-fed mutton, barn-door fowls, pies, milk-cheese etc. all in perfection; and so much simplicity resides among these hills, that a pen, which could write at least, was not to be found about the house, till I shot the crow with whose quill I wrote this epistle.'

Alternatively, to short-cut the loop to Langlee, stay close to the wall when the track pulls away from it and descend on access land. Keep left and follow a path through a gate, then head for a stout drystone wall. Turn right to follow this downhill, and cross a couple of stiles to reach a narrow footbridge over **Harthope Burn**. Climb to a road and turn right across a bridge over **Hawsen Burn**.

Climb from a circular sheepfold, either using a steep and narrow heathery path, or a slightly less steep grassy path. Either way, turn left along the most well trodden path across the heathery slopes well above **Hawsen Burn**. This path eventually joins a stony track.

Turn right to follow it further up the valley, and keep straight ahead to avoid another track and path heading left. Cross a broad, heathery gap, passing a stile beside a gate, then head downhill.

When the track swings markedly down to the right, leave it to walk straight ahead along a moorland path, roughly contouring across the lower slopes of **Broadhope Hill**. A marker post bears both footpath and bridleway arrows, so be sure to turn right as marked for the

A forest track is fringed by yellow broom as it climbs above Carey Burn to reach Wooler Common

bridleway, to reach a track near the isolated house of **Broadstruther**. (The high-level Day 7 route joins at this point.) Pass the cottage and follow the track downhill, but watch for a path heading left down to a footbridge.

Climb from the bridge to pass a stile by a gate, then continue straight ahead across a rugged slope well above the river. Go through a gate into what the map shows as forest, but which is mostly bracken and broom.

Head downhill and cross a footbridge over **Carey Burn**, then turn right to walk downstream. A marker post shows where the path later climbs from the river, as a delightful green ribbon on an otherwise rugged slope. Go through a gate and a gentler ascent continues over moorland.

Turn right along a broad and stony track, following it downhill through a gate to approach buildings at **Wooler Common**. Turn left and right to pass the buildings as signposted, then later turn left down a grassy path to reach a marker post for St Cuthbert's Way. Head up to a small gate and go into a forest to follow a grassy path straight uphill.

Veer slightly right to head downhill, and later go through a gate to leave the forest. A grassy path leads downhill and a gate leads to **Waud House**. Turn left down the access road, then turn right along another road and follow it into the Market Place in the centre of **Wooler.** (For facilities, see the end of Day 7 main route, page 95.)

DAY 8

Wooler to Bamburgh via Belford

Start	Wooler – NT994283
Finish	Bamburgh – NU181349
Distance	29 km (18 miles)
Maps	OS Landranger 75 or OS Explorer 340
Terrain	Mostly easy roads, tracks and paths in gentle countryside.
Refreshments	Plenty of choice at Belford and Bamburgh.
Public Transport	Regular daily Arriva and Travelsure buses serve Belford from Berwick-upon-Tweed, Alnwick, and Newcastle. Buses also link Belford with Waren Mill, Bamburgh and other places along the coast.

There are two routes from Wooler to Bamburgh. The most direct option is the original course of the Reivers Way, as described by Harold Wade, while a longer alternative, via Chillingham, was offered by James Roberts (see Day 8 Alternative in this guidebook). The direct route is, at least in its early stages, signposted as St Cuthbert's Way, and followed almost to St Cuthbert's Cave. This day's walk can be broken early at Belford, otherwise keep walking to the coast, with a view to reaching the delightful village of Bamburgh.

Leave the parish church in **Wooler** by walking down Church Street, as signposted for St Cuthbert's Way. Cross the busy **A697** at the bottom, walk straight along Weetwood Road and cross a bridge over Wooler Water.

Turn right to walk through a green space behind a long row of houses, then turn left along another road and pass a **school**. Keep straight ahead along the road, away from town, climbing uphill to reach a pronounced bend.

Turn left as signposted up Weetwood Moor Lane, which is a narrow path in a deep groove, eventually reaching a gate leading onto the open slopes of **Weetwood Moor**.

The path climbs past bracken and heather with the sandstone bedrock occasionally revealed. Enjoy fine views back to the Cheviots, but watch for marker posts on the broad top of the moor, around 150m (490ft). A broad and grassy path passes a cairn and runs alongside a ruined drystone wall.

Go through a gate and pass a small forest. Later, turn left through a gate beside another small forest. When the far corner of the forest is reached, head diagonally right to reach a stile.

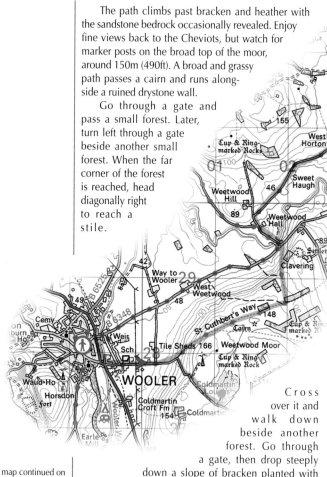

Cross over it and walk down beside another forest. Go through a gate, then drop steeply down a slope of bracken planted with young trees, aiming for a road junction.

Cross the weak stone arch of **Weetwood Bridge** and follow the road onwards and uphill, bending right to take an undulating course to Hortons. **West Horton** and **East Horton** lie side by side and are small farming hamlets.

map continued on page 108

● Day 8 Alternative

Turn left up a road as signposted for St Cuthbert's Way and Lowick.

Turn right up a farm access road, later heading down past a concrete pillbox. Continue down a track and turn left, rising a little. The track runs downhill to cross a wooden bridge over **Hetton Burn**, then climbs to a road junction beside an old school converted to a dwelling.

Walk straight ahead along the road signposted for Belford and marked as St Cuthbert's Way. The road later climbs and has a stand of pines to the left, where a road joins from the right, near **Old Hazelrigg.** (Walkers who follow the Day 8 Alternative route from Wooler have a link back to this direct route at this point – see Link from Chatton to Day 8 direct route, page 120.) A little further uphill, go through a gate on the left and follow a grassy path to link with a track.

Go through a gate on the right and turn left to walk along the bottom edge of a large field, to reach a stile beside a gate. Cross the stile and walk straight ahead down to a gate and cross-tracks. Turn right up another track, then at the top, turn right to leave St Cuthbert's Way and continue along the Reivers Way. ▸

The Reivers Way follows a forest track onto a shoulder of **Cockenheugh**, around 150m (490ft). Go through a gate to follow a grassy track gently downhill. Go through another gate and rise gently past some old buildings at **Dick's Oldwalls**, then head downhill again. Turn right to pass a large complex of farm buildings to reach a horse-riding centre at **Swinhoe Farm**.

Go through a kissing-gate and walk up to a mobile phone mast to find another kissing-gate behind it. The route being followed is marked 'Coast Path', despite being a long way from the coast. However, make use of the waymarks while following the path alongside a gentle crest overlooking fields and farms.

Turn left, however, to detour a little off-route to a nearby Scots pine plantation, then turn right uphill to visit St Cuthbert's Cave beneath a gritstone crag.

Cross a farm access road serving **Craggyhall**, but continue as marked straight along a path from field to field. Turn left as marked later, crossing an old stone dam near the pele tower of **Westhall**. A streamside path leads to a road, where walkers turn right, then later turn left to enter **Belford**.

BELFORD

Belford has reverted to a quiet village since being bypassed by the main A1. There is a fine paved area and an old stone cross in the middle of the village. The Blue Bell Hotel faces the cross and there are other lodgings, as well as Bluebell Farm and its bunk-barn. There is a post office, a couple of pubs, a supermarket with an ATM, a take-away and a café. Regular daily Arriva and Travelsure buses link Belford with Berwick-upon-Tweed, Alnwick and Newcastle, while others head for Bamburgh and Seahouses on the coast.

Follow the main road south, passing Belford Hall, then turn left at the Belford, where a golf course has a café/bar open to the public. Walk between the trickle of **Belford Burn** and a tall fence alongside a golf driving range.

Continue through a field and cross the busy **A1** with great care. Pass several huge, cylindrical metal silos at the Coastal Grains complex. (Compare and contrast these with the granaries built by the Romans at Housesteads!)

Head towards another prominent Coastal Grains silo, and the path reaches a busy, high-speed railway line.

map continued on page 110

A complex of massive grain silos is passed as the Reivers Way heads from Belford to the coast

109

A **telephone** is provided so that you can call the signalman to ensure that it is safe to cross. Tell him you are at 'Belford Crossing', proceed only when told it is safe, do not linger on the line, and ensure that the gates are closed afterwards.

The path soon crosses a disused quarry railway, then continues, marked 'Coast Path', along an old quarry road before running through fields. To spot the exact course of the route ahead, simply trace the overhead power line running through fields to reach a road.

Turn left to follow the road down and up towards **Chesterhill**, then turn right as indicated by a signpost to follow a field path. Keep to the left of a wooded valley, walking beside fields before heading down to a road at **Waren Mill**. Turn left to reach a road junction, then turn right to follow the **B1342** along the coast of **Budle Bay**.

WAREN MILL

Waren Mill was first mentioned in 1187, and by 1605 the mill race was noted as being derelict. The large mill buildings were built by the Admiralty in 1783, as local farmers needed storage and shipment facilities for their wheat. A steam engine was installed in 1819 and the building was enlarged in 1831, only to be burnt down in 1881. It was restored two years later, more machinery was installed in 1913, while maltings were added in 1924. The whole edifice has been converted into apartments overlooking the mudflats and marshes of the Lindisfarne and Budle Bay National Nature Reserve. The Waren House Hotel is a short way inland, and there are nearby campsites and bus services.

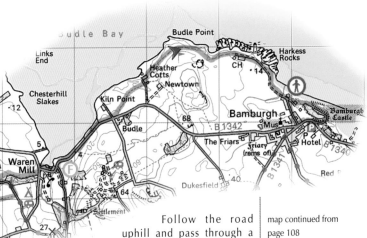

Follow the road uphill and pass through a crossroads at **Budle**, then go through a gate on the left. Cross a field diagonally, passing a gateway, then follow a ruined drystone wall towards some mobile homes. Watch for a small gate leading onto a narrow road, and turn left to follow the road down past the restored **Heather Cottages**.

Don't go down to the beach, but follow a narrow path behind dunes covered in spiky marram grass. Climb past a concrete structure to find a bridleway signposted along the top of the dunes. The path becomes broader as it passes a golf course overlooking **Budle Point**. ▶ Follow blue marker posts past the club house, then follow a road past **Harkness Rocks**.

On reaching the outskirts of **Bamburgh** there are two options. If the feet are weary after the long day's walk, then stay on the road to enter the village. If a little more energy can be summoned, it is worth turning left along a track, then following paths through dunes covered in marram grass and ivy.

The path runs beside an old fence, and simply keeps seawards of the crags supporting **Bamburgh Castle**, until the castle access road is reached. Double back into **Bamburgh** by road if a night is to be spent in the village.

map continued from page 108

The distant island of Lindisfarne and the rugged, rocky Farne Islands are in view.

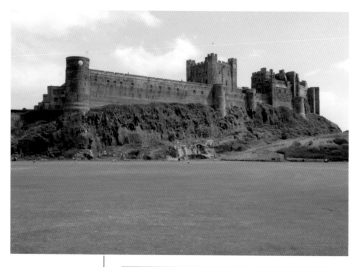

Bamburgh Castle largely dates from 1894, dominates Bamburgh village, and is home to the Armstrong family

BAMBURGH

Bamburgh is derived from Bebbanburg, or 'the Rock of Bebba', who was a sixth-century Saxon queen. The delightful village is arranged around a well-wooded central green and has plenty of interest. A museum dedicated to Grace Darling faces a church founded by St Aidan. The village has hotels and other lodgings, as well as a number of pubs, restaurants, tea rooms and shops. Arriva and Travelsure buses head inland to Belford and onwards to Berwick-upon-Tweed, as well as running along the coast before heading inland to Alnwick for Newcastle.

BAMBURGH CASTLE

The craggy outcrop of the Whin Sill at Bamburgh has been fortified since ancient times, and in 547AD, Ida 'the Flamebearer' built a wooden fort there. Various structures have been raised and levelled through centuries of strife and changes of ownership, but it has generally been regarded as an important royal site. The current castle is a rather fanciful structure dating largely from 1894, and originally planned as a convalescent home for retired gentlemen. The developer was the Victorian inventor and engineer Lord Armstrong of Cragside House, Rothbury. He died before it was completed and the castle is now inhabited by the Armstrong family. It is open daily from 10am to 5pm, March to October, and includes a museum and tea room. There is an entry charge, tel 01668 214515, www.bamburghcastle.com.

ST OSWALD AND ST AIDAN

Oswald was born in 605AD and reigned as king of Northumbria from 633AD to 642AD. Although of pagan Anglo-Saxon lineage, he was a Christian, and spent some time with the remote Celtic Christian community on the Scottish island of Iona. Oswald's base was Bamburgh, though he travelled extensively, and united remarkably different tribes, regardless of language and cultural differences, encouraging the spread of Christianity throughout the region. In 635 AD he invited Aidan, an Irish bishop from Iona, to assist him.

Aidan founded a monastic community at Lindisfarne and travelled extensively around Northumbria, preaching and converting people, while Oswald lent his authority and helped with translation. Under Oswald, Northumbria became a large and powerful kingdom, but he met his death in battle against a long-standing enemy, the pagan ruler Penda, at Shrewsbury in 642AD. Oswald's body was mutilated and he was deemed to be a martyr. Aidan continued travelling and preaching until 651AD when, heading back to Lindisfarne, he suffered an illness and died in a tent pitched against the church he had founded at Bamburgh.

GRACE DARLING

The story of Grace Darling is connected with the Farne Islands, but she was born in Bambugh in 1815 and buried there in 1842. Soon after birth, Grace

The Longstone was Grace Darling's home in 1838, when she helped rescue survivors from the Forfarshire

was taken to Brownsman Island where her father, William, operated a basic lighthouse. When a new lighthouse was built on the Longstone, the family moved there in 1826. Most of Grace's siblings had left home by 1838, when one stormy September morning she saw the wreck of the paddle-steamer *Forfarshire* on the nearby Big Harcar. Later she noticed survivors clinging to the rock. William Darling reckoned the sea was too rough to attempt a rescue. Grace not only persuaded him to go, but accompanied him on the first of two dangerous trips to save nine survivors. It was two days later that the sea was calm enough for them to be taken to the mainland.

Grace Darling became a national heroine at the age of 22, fêted by the press, awarded medals for bravery, sitting for portraits, receiving gifts and even marriage proposals from admirers. She didn't particularly relish her 'celebrity' status. Sadly, she contracted tuberculosis and died in the arms of her father in 1842. Her funeral was a huge affair, and an impressive monument was erected over her grave in St Aidan's churchyard two years later. A museum dedicated to her memory was opened in Bamburgh and the RNLI has recently renewed it completely, tel 01668 214910, www.rnli.org.uk/gracedarling.

DAY 8 ALTERNATIVE

Wooler to Bamburgh via Chillingham

Start	Wooler – NT994283
Finish	Bamburgh – NU181349
Distance	31km (19 miles)
Maps	OS Landrangers 75 and 81 or OS Explorers 332 and 340
Terrain	Mostly easy roads, tracks and paths in gentle countryside.
Refreshments	Pubs at Chatton, Warenford, Lucker and Bamburgh.
Public Transport	Occasional Travelsure buses from Wooler serve Chatton, Chillingham and Alnwick. Regular daily Arriva buses link Warenford with Alnwick, Belford and Berwick-upon-Tweed. Regular daily Arriva and Travelsure buses link Waren Mill with Belford, Bamburgh and the coast.

There are two routes from Wooler to Bamburgh, and this longer alternative was created by James Roberts for walkers who wish to visit Chillingham. Think carefully before heading for Chillingham Castle and the Wild Cattle Park, as an exploration of both places takes a few hours, and it might not be possible to walk all the way to Bamburgh afterwards. Consider an overnight at Chatton, or continue onwards and break the journey at Warenford.

Leave the parish church in **Wooler** by walking down Church Street, as signposted for St Cuthbert's Way. Cross the busy **A697** at the bottom, walk straight along Weetwood Road and cross a bridge over Wooler Water.

Turn right to walk through a green space behind a long row of houses, then turn left along another road and pass a **school**. Keep straight ahead along the road, away from town, climbing uphill round a pronounced bend.

Climb to the very crest of the road where the tarmac ends at around 150m (490ft). An ugly girder-work radio mast stands well away to the left on **Weetwood Moor**.

Follow a fine enclosed track onwards, enjoying views back to the Cheviot Hills. The track is a broad, grassy strip

map continued on page 122

as it later runs across a huge field where boulders have been cleared and stacked alongside. A short footpath is available for anyone who wants to inspect a nearby ancient hilltop enclosure, otherwise simply follow the track onwards to reach a cottage and a house.

Walk along the access road, heading downhill with a view of **Lilburn Tower** to the right. Go

straight through a crossroads and follow the road up through the hamlet of **Newtown**, briefly along the course of the old Roman road of Devil's Causeway.

Turn left at a junction and walk down the road to cross a stone-arch bridge over the **River Till**. A tree-lined avenue leads to the entrance gates to **Chillingham Castle**, where occasional buses pass.

CHILLINGHAM CASTLE

It takes time to visit Chillingham Castle properly, so if this option is taken, it is best to split this long day's walk by staying a night at nearby Chatton.

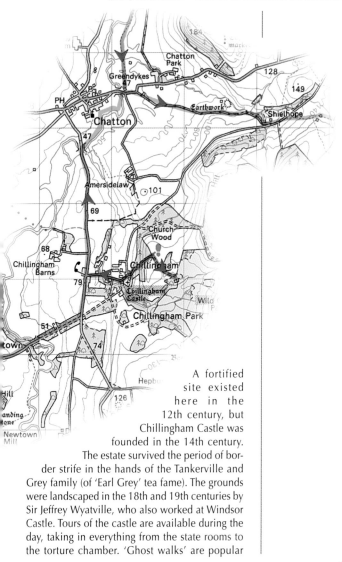

A fortified site existed here in the 12th century, but Chillingham Castle was founded in the 14th century. The estate survived the period of border strife in the hands of the Tankerville and Grey family (of 'Earl Grey' tea fame). The grounds were landscaped in the 18th and 19th centuries by Sir Jeffrey Wyatville, who also worked at Windsor Castle. Tours of the castle are available during the day, taking in everything from the state rooms to the torture chamber. 'Ghost walks' are popular

The statue is of Field Marshall Viscount Gough (1779–1869). Originally in Dublin, it was repeatedly vandalised and even exploded. In 1988 it was acquired (and restored) by the current resident of the Castle, a distant relative of Gough.

in the evenings, and the castle claims to be the most haunted in Britain! There is an entry charge, tel 01668 215359, www.chillingham-castle.com. The castle can be hired for weddings and other functions and also features a tea room.

If not visiting **Chillingham Castle**, turn left at the road junction to walk along the road to the nearby village of **Chillingham**, passing a bronze statue on horseback. ◀

There is an option to turn right in the village, either to visit St Peter's Church, or to see the famous Chillingham wild cattle.

CHILLINGHAM WILD CATTLE

A solitary bull from the famous herd of wild cattle enclosed since 1270 within Chillingham Park

The white, long-horned 'wild cattle' were enclosed within the walls of Chillingham Park in 1270, and have little interaction with people, least of all border reivers! Herd records date only from 1692, but make interesting reading. In the bitter winter of 1947, numbers fell as low as 13, while in 1967 and 2001, foot-and-mouth disease outbreaks occurred

very close to the park. The entire herd was at risk on those occasions, so a reserve herd has been established at a secret location in Scotland, and it is hoped to preserve frozen semen and embryos against future disaster. The herd and the park were held for centuries by Chillingham Castle, but are now owned and managed by the Chillingham Wild Cattle Association.

Walkers must spare up to 1½ hours to be escorted into Chillingham Park by the warden. Visits take place from April to October, usually twice daily, except Tuesdays. There is an entry charge, tel 01668 215250, www.chillingham-wildcattle.org.uk. To reach the start of a tour from the church, follow the track marked 'Forest Walks' to the top of the hill. Go through a gate and turn right, then head diagonally down through a field to find the warden at a stone byre.

Follow the road away from the village of **Chillingham** and cross the **River Till**. The road could be followed straight to the village of **Chatton**, but it is also possible to cross a stile on the right and avoid the village altogether by following the river downstream through a couple of fields to reach a triple-arched stone bridge. This isn't a right of way, but access is available under the Countryside Stewardship Scheme.

CHATTON

Facilities include the Percy Arms Hotel, the Old Manse guest house, village store and post office, as well as a gallery and a fine central green. Occasional Travelsure buses run between Wooler, Chatton, Chillingham and Alnwick. A curious metal monument erected in the year 2000 turns out to represent a plan of the road system in the village.

LINK FROM CHATTON TO DAY 8 MAIN ROUTE

This link is for those who, having visited Chillingham, now wish to return to the direct course of the Reivers Way to reach Belford.

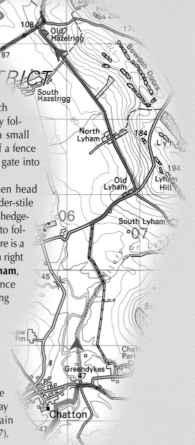

Cross the triple-arched stone bridge, then turn left to follow a public footpath past a playing field. A field path runs parallel to the **River Till**, but well away from the flow. Watch for a stile over a fence, closely followed by a footbridge over a small stream. Keep to the left side of a fence to return to the **River Till** at a gate into a field.

Walk beside the river, then head away from it and cross a ladder-stile onto a grassy track flanked by hedgerows at **Lyham Burn**. Turn left to follow this track to the **B6349** (there is a schoolday bus to Wooler). Turn right up the road to pass **Old Lyham**, with a view of Lyham Hill, once one of best millstone quarrying sites in the county.

Turn left along a minor road to pass **North Lyham**. Follow the road onwards, passing **Old Hazelrigg** just before reaching a road junction. Turn right to regain the direct course of the Reivers Way at this point (see Day 8 main route, **Old Hazelrigg**, page 107).

To stay on the alternative route, cross the triple-arched stone bridge outside **Chatton**, then take the second 'no through road' on the right. ▸

This narrow tarmac road has a fishery to the right, then the site of an 18th-century tile-works and a Bronze Age settlement to the left.

The end of the road is reached at **Shielhope**, where there are two gates. Go through the gate on the right and turn left up a grassy track. Keep right to go through gates at some sheep pens, then follow a fence to the top of a rugged field. Go through gates and keep straight ahead beside another fence to pass the tumbled ruins of **Coalhouses**.

Follow a fence onwards and squeeze past gorse bushes to cross a small stream and go through a gate. Walk up a bracken slope to reach a solitary tree and look ahead across **Chatton Moor**. Use any trodden path to get down to a fence that has a path running parallel, below a low crag.

Pass in front of the ruined farm at Brownridge, then pick up a good track leading easily across a rugged moor

Aim for a metal chest on wheels, then turn right to see two grassy tracks splitting apart. Take the one on the left, over the moors, passing clumps of gorse. The track forks, so keep right to reach the right-hand corner of a forest, where the ruined farm of **Brownridge** is seen.

A track leads through forest, fording Sandyford Burn on its way to Twizell and Twizell House

Go in front of the farm to pass it, then cross a step-stile and go through a gate. Go through another gate onto bleak moor-land,

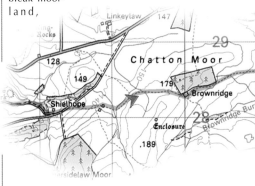

fortunately boasting a good, firm grassy track all the way across. Pass through a couple more gates to reach a large barn beside a forest.

Go through a gate, then walk along and down a forest track, fording **Sandyford Burn**. Follow the track uphill and left, then down to a ford and footbridge. Walk up a road to pass houses at **Twizell**, then at the last farm building, turn right down a track into woodland.

When a track junction is reached, follow a grassy track as signposted. Turn left towards **Twizell House**, then right and left to walk down through the woods. Watch for marker posts, turning left up towards the house, then walk along a track with railings alongside. Looking back towards the house, notice the 'ha-ha' wall between the lawn and fields.

Walk downhill to pass under a concrete bridge carrying the busy **A1**, then head out of the woods into the village of **Warenford**. Either walk straight ahead by road, or turn right for the White

map continued on page 124

Swan Inn. There are regular daily Arriva buses to Alnwick, Belford and Berwick-upon-Tweed.

Pass the Old Manse, then go through a gate on the right and walk the full length of a field to find a gate. Cross a wooden bridge spanning **Waren Burn**. Turn left to walk along the edge of a field, beside the wooded river valley. Walkers are supposed to go through a gate on the left, in a field corner, but the path heading downstream becomes quite difficult in places, and some prefer to continue along the edge of the fields instead.

Whatever route is chosen, the path finally approaches some buildings. Before reaching them, turn right to cross a stile, then turn left to follow a road into the village of **Lucker**, where the Apple Inn is located.

Across the road from the inn, a footpath signpost points further downstream beside **Waren Burn**. The riverbanks are wooded, but the path climbs a little to continue along the edge of a field. The stream leads to a railway bridge, where the path is supported on a metal grid to pass beneath the railway, but above the water. Watch carefully, while crossing a large field, to spot a grassed-over bridge spanning a drain, then head up to a stile onto the **B1341**. Cross the road and cross another stile, then walk alongside a couple of big fields. Cross a road and pass between buildings at **Bradford**.

Walk alongside another field, then go through a gate and walk down a forested slope. Cross a footbridge over a stream, then climb and turn left, but quickly swing right up a forested slope. Go through a gate into a field, then continue straight ahead alongside a hedgerow. A gate leads onto the corner of a road at **Spindlestone**.

map continued from page 123

See map on page 111 for remainder of route.

A large building at Waren Mill has been converted into apartments overlooking Budle Bay

Walk straight ahead and down the road to reach a mill and a bridge over **Waren Burn**. Don't cross the bridge, but turn right along a road, passing Waren House Hotel to reach the little village of **Waren Mill**. Turn right to follow the **B1342** along the coast of **Budle Bay**.

WAREN MILL

Waren Mill was first mentioned in 1187, and by 1605 the mill race was noted as being derelict. The large mill buildings were built by the Admiralty in 1783, as local farmers needed storage and shipment facilities for their wheat. A steam engine was installed in 1819 and the building was enlarged in 1831, only

125

to be burnt down in 1881. It was restored two years later, more machinery was installed in 1913, while maltings were added in 1924. The whole edifice has been converted into apartments overlooking the mudflats and marshes of the Lindisfarne and Budle Bay National Nature Reserve. The Waren House Hotel is a short way inland, and there are nearby campsites and bus services.

Follow the road uphill and pass through a crossroads at **Budle**, then go through a gate on the left. Cross a field diagonally, passing a gateway, then follow a ruined dry-stone wall towards some mobile homes. Watch for a small gate leading onto a narrow road, and turn left to follow the road down past the restored **Heather Cottages**.

Don't go down to the beach, but follow a narrow path behind dunes covered in spiky marram grass. Climb past a concrete structure to find a bridleway signposted along the top of the dunes. The path becomes broader as it passes a golf course overlooking **Budle Point**. ◀

The distant island of Lindisfarne and the rugged, rocky Farne Islands are in view.

Follow blue marker posts past the club house, then follow a road past **Harkness Rocks**.

On reaching the outskirts of **Bamburgh** there are two options. If the feet are weary after the long day's walk, then stay on the road to enter the village. If a little more energy can be summoned, it is worth turning left along a track, then following paths through dunes covered in marram grass and ivy.

The path runs beside an old fence and simply keeps seawards of the crags supporting **Bamburgh Castle**, until the castle access road is reached. Double back into **Bamburgh** by road if a night is to be spent in the village (for facilities, see the end of the Day 8 direct route, page 112).

DAY 9

Bamburgh to Alnmouth

Start	Bamburgh – NU81349
Finish	Alnmouth – NU246105
Distance	31km (19 miles)
Maps	OS Landrangers 75 and 81 or OS Explorers 332 and 340
Terrain	Easy coastal roads, tracks and paths, but sometimes set well back from the sea. Sandy beach walks may be available at low water.
Refreshments	Pubs and/or cafés available at Seahouses, Beadnell, Dunstanburgh golf course, Craster, Boulmer and Alnmouth.
Public Transport	Regular daily Travelsure buses link most coastal villages, while Arriva buses link coastal villages with Berwick-upon-Tweed, Alnwick and Newcastle. Summer ferries operate from Seahouses to the Farne Islands.

The final stage on the Reivers Way is entirely along the Northumberland coast. While a 'coastal path' has been waymarked, it occasionally wanders inland, but most of the time it is possible to stride along a sandy shore. This is a long day's walk with many points of interest, so feel free to break the journey and cover the distance over two days. If a boat trip to the Farne Islands is included, then an extra day will certainly be needed.

HERRING GIRLS

While trekking along the Northumberland coast, you will be walking in the footsteps of the 'Herring Girls'. During the peak years of the herring fishing industry, when huge shoals of 'silver darlings' migrated along the coast, fishing boats would follow them and land enormous catches. Onshore, gangs of itinerant girls would keep pace with the fishermen, ready to gut and split the herrings, earning an enviable wage at the time, although admittedly it was hard work. Some girls would trek along both the Scottish and

English coasts throughout the season, while others would work along a shorter stretch of coast, returning home soon afterwards. The days of the 'Herring Girls' are over, and machines can split around 500kg (half a ton) of herrings in an hour.

Bamburgh Dunes is a designated site of special scientific interest, and its flowers include pyramidal orchids and centuary.

Leave **Bamburgh** by following the B1340 along the coast (using the pavement). ◄

Flowery sand dunes south of Bamburgh are managed as a nature reserve and lead to a sandy shore

If tidal conditions allow, follow a path across the dunes and walk along the shore, which is variously sandy or rocky and offers good views of the Farne Islands. **Monkshouse**, hemmed between the coast road and the sandy shore, was the site of a storehouse built to accommodate goods in transit to the Farne Islands, for the use of early Christian hermits.

Whichever route is taken, follow the coast road into the bustling resort of **Seahouses**.

SEAHOUSES

Seahouses developed from a small fishing harbour, diversifying into shipping lime from kilns at North Sunderland from 1770 to 1860. The village's growth into a tourist resort was initially fuelled by the Grace Darling story

map continued on page 132

Islestone 35

27

Greenhill Rocks

Monks Ho

Monks House Rocks

New Shoreston

Shoreston Hall

5

St Aidan's Dunes

The Tumblers

Carr End

LB Sta

Breakwater

Seahouses

Springhill

16

Cemy

Mus

Braidcarr Point

West Field Fm

PH

Sch

P

Cemy

North Sunderland

14

Snook or North Sunderland Point

CH

Annstead Fm

Annstead Rocks

24

Linkhouse

from the 1840s, increased following the construction of the North Sunderland Railway in 1898, then developed apace from 1930. The railway ran until 1951, but its closure has not affected the popularity of the place.

The outer wall of the harbour was built in the 1880s to accommodate an expanding herring fleet, whose peak years were from 1830 to 1930. The humble

Monkshouse, between Bamburgh and Seahouses, was once a shipment point for hermits on the Farne Islands

'kipper' was invented at Seahouses. According to legend, split herrings were accidentally left in a shed where a fire was burning overnight, flavouring the fish with smoke. According to fact, John Woodger developed the 'kippering' process in 1843.

Seahouses has a full range of services, the greatest on the whole of the Reivers Way, including abundant accommodation, banks with ATMs, post office, plenty of shops, pubs, restaurants and take-aways, not to mention amusement arcades. There is a National Trust shop, the Seahouses Heritage Museum, boat trips to the Farne Islands, and regular daily buses to other coastal villages. There is a tourist information centre, tel 01665 720884.

Walk through the centre of **Seahouses** and head down to the harbour, then walk round the harbour by road and continue as signposted for the coast path. Follow marker posts across a **golf course**, which soon direct walkers straight inland from low cliffs to reach the **B1340**.

Turn left to follow a broad tarmac footpath and cycleway beside the road all the way to **Beadnell**. Alternatively, use any of the access paths leading onto a belt of dunes between the sea and the road, then walk along the beach. Remember that the dunes are managed as a nature reserve and shouldn't be trodden too much.

BEADNELL

Beadnell village is set a little inland from tiny Beadnell harbour, where an impressive complex of big limekilns is owned by the National Trust. Facilities include accommodation, post office shop, pub and coffee shop. Regular daily buses link Beadnell with other coastal villages as well as Berwick-upon-Tweed, Alnwick and Newcastle.

There is no need to follow the road all the way to the **Beadnell harbour** (or if you do, retrace steps), but turn right as signposted for a car park instead. Continue along the access road for Beadnell Bay caravan park, then, at

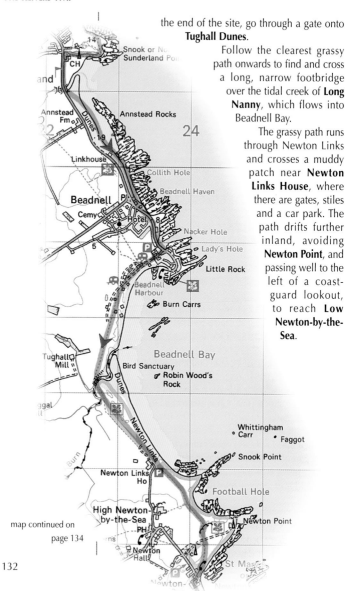

the end of the site, go through a gate onto **Tughall Dunes**.

Follow the clearest grassy path onwards to find and cross a long, narrow footbridge over the tidal creek of **Long Nanny**, which flows into Beadnell Bay.

The grassy path runs through Newton Links and crosses a muddy patch near **Newton Links House**, where there are gates, stiles and a car park. The path drifts further inland, avoiding **Newton Point**, and passing well to the left of a coast-guard lookout, to reach **Low Newton-by-the-Sea**.

map continued on page 134

LOW NEWTON-BY-THE-SEA

The Ship Inn at Low Newton is part of an arrange-
ment of buildings standing around three sides of a
courtyard green facing the sea, in the care of the
National Trust. Nearby Newton Pool, held behind a
belt of grassy dunes, is managed as a nature reserve
and equipped with bird-hides.

Walk round the back of the buildings at **Low Newton**
to follow a track, then keep left of a house to pick up a
path that passes Newton Pool. A jumble of huts is scattered among the grassy dunes, so fork right at a path
junction as marked to avoid most of them, and later walk
beside a **golf course**.

When the club house comes into view, walk across a
narrow part of the golf course towards it. ▸

Turn left to hug the landward perimeter of the golf
course and eventually reach **Dunstanburgh Castle**.

DUNSTANBURGH CASTLE

This castle is an iconic scene on the Northumberland
coast, and described as 'Thomas of Lancaster's majes-
tic stronghold'. It dates from 1314 and had little to

*Whitewashed cottages
and the Ship Inn are
arranged round a
square green at Low
Newton-by-the-Sea*

Food and drink are
available at the club
house, as well as
access to the village
of Embleton and all
its services further
inland.

133

do with defending the area against raiders and reivers. The castle guarded a small harbour, of which little trace remains, and may well have been raised to challenge the authority of King Edward II. Dunstanburgh saw action during the Wars of the Roses in the 1460s. It was severely damaged at that time and never repaired, so that by 1538 it was described as a 'very reuynus howsse and of smalle strength.' After being plundered for stone and exposed to the elements, the most impressive remains are the drum towers flanking the entrance gate. The castle is open daily through the summer from 10am to 5pm, but closed on Tuesdays and Wednesdays in winter. There is an entrance charge, tel 01665 576231, www.english-heritage. org.uk.

Set off from Dunstanburgh Castle and follow a broad, smooth, easy and popular path to the village of **Craster**. Walk on past the little harbour.

Boats pulled high above the little harbour at Craster

CRASTER

Craster kippers enjoy an excellent reputation, so literally follow your nose to a smokehouse. There is a shop and restaurant on site, www.kipper.co.uk. The Jolly Fisherman Inn stands opposite and has an ATM. There is also a tearoom and shop in the village, as well as a little accommodation. Regular daily buses link Craster with other coastal villages.

Keep seawards of the Jolly Fisherman Inn to leave **Craster**, passing through a beer garden to pick up the coast path. A grassy path leaves the village and eventually turns right on **Cullernose Point**. Look back to see fine cliffs, used as a nesting site by kittiwakes, then almost land on a road near **Howick**. ▶

Walk parallel to the road, passing the solitary Bathing House, lovingly restored from dereliction. Beautiful sandy beaches and jumbled cliffs are passed at **Rumbling Kern**. Further along the coast there is a wooded area and a sandy beach at **Howick Haven**, where a concrete footbridge spans a river.

Cross the footbridge and climb up a clear path, later passing a road-end with a gate. The village of

An emergency telephone here advises dialling 999, but has only a single button labelled 1!

135

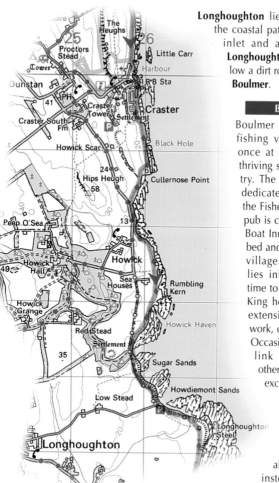

Longhoughton lies inland. Keep to the coastal path to cross a sandy inlet and a footbridge near **Longhoughton Steel**, then follow a dirt road to the village of **Boulmer**.

BOULMER

Boulmer is very much a fishing village that was once at the centre of a thriving smuggling industry. The little church is dedicated to St Andrew the Fisherman, while the pub is called the Fishing Boat Inn, and there is a bed and breakfast in the village. RAF Boulmer lies inland, and from time to time yellow Sea King helicopters, used extensively for rescue work, can be observed. Occasional Arriva buses link Boulmer with other coastal villages, except Sundays.

Follow the road through **Boulmer**, but when it turns inland, continue along the coast path instead. Pass through an area being restored to its original dune flora and reach an area where a few caravans are scattered around **Seaton Point**. This is a private site operated by the Seaton Point Caravan Association.

map continued on page 137

Turn right to follow a grassy track towards **Seaton House**, then, as the last farm building is reached, turn left along a track, then later right along a path, to get back to the coast. However, there is a risk of reaching an impasse here, where steps descend to the sandy beach and progress is dependent on the state of the tide. Normally, there will be no problem walking 750m (½ mile) along the beach, but if the tide is high, then it may be necessary to wait until it recedes a little.

Follow the beach until houses are reached at **Fluke Hole**, and a gate reveals a path running up to a golf course. Pass the club house at **Foxton Hall** and turn left, then walk as indicated by marker posts. Pass a wooded patch, then cross the golf course to head up a grassy path flanked by bracken and brambles. Turn left at an old battery and walk down a grooved path, reaching a road on **Alnmouth Common**.

map continued on page 139

Walk straight ahead as signposted for Alnmouth, crossing the last part of the golf course. Simply follow roads

The Reivers Way ends at the village of Alnmouth, but can be continued inland to a railway station

into the middle of **Alnmouth** to declare the Reivers Way finished at a convenient pub or bus stop. Alternatively, follow the **B1338** out of the village, crossing the tidal **River Aln** and the A1068, and climb uphill to reach **Alnwick with Alnmouth Station**.

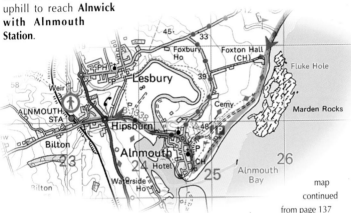

map
continued
from page 137

ALNMOUTH

Alnmouth was built as a 'new town' in 1150, shipping grain and building ships at the mouth of the River Aln. Looking across the river mouth, views take in Coquet Island. The Schooner Hotel claims to be the most haunted hotel in the country. Facilities include a good range of accommodation, post office, shops, pubs and restaurants. Regular daily Arriva buses link Alnmouth with other coastal villages, as well as heading inland to the railway station, Alnwick and Newcastle, for onward travel.

THE FARNE
ISLANDS

The Farne Islands are small, low-lying, rough and rocky, and all part of the Whin Sill that outcrops so extensively around Northumberland. Depending on the state of the tide and the definition of an 'island', there might be 28 in the archipelago. The islands are famous for supporting up to 100,000 pairs of breeding seabirds and a colony of nearly 4000 grey seals. Early Christian hermits used them as retreats, most notably St Cuthbert in the seventh century. Eider ducks are referred to locally as 'Cuddy's ducks' in honour of St Cuthbert. Thousands of puffins jostle alongside guillemots, shags and razorbills, while raucous arctic and sandwich terns peck at visitors who get too close to their nests. Kittiwakes and other members of the gull family are also present.

The National Trust has owned and managed the Farne Islands since 1925. Access is allowed to Inner Farne and Staple Island, and landing fees must be paid by anyone who isn't a National Trust member. Visits are popular with bird-watchers, who haul impressive cameras, lenses and scopes ashore. Landings are also permitted on the Longstone, which is a property of Trinity House. There is no landing fee, but there is a charge for visiting the lighthouse.

Anyone breaking their walk around the Reivers Way to visit the Farne Islands will need to

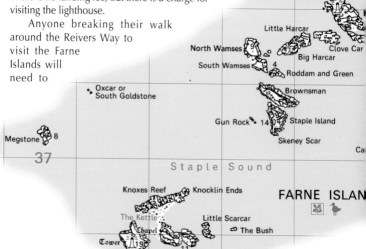

140

Long queues at Seahouses ensure that boat trips to the
Farne Islands fill up very quickly in the summertime

stone

allow an extra day on the Northumberland coast. Sailings generally
commence at 10.30am in the summer, but hectic queues form at the
ticket kiosks and the boats fill quickly. It is a good idea to phone a day
or two in advance and reserve a place. A simple cruise around the
islands takes 1½ hours. Landings are possible on three islands, allowing one hour ashore in addition to the cruise time. Rarely, it is possible
to land on two or even three islands on the same trip, but these outings
last up to six hours. Bear in mind that sailings and landings are dependent
on the weather and tidal conditions.

Boat Trip Operators
- Four ticket kiosks are located beside the harbour at
  Seahouses.
- Billy Shiels, tel 01665 720308, www.farne-islands.com
- Hanvey's, tel 01665 720388, www.farneislands.co.uk
- Sovereign, tel 01665 720059, www.sovereigndiving.co.uk
- Golden Gate, tel 01665 721210, www.farneislandsboattrips.co.uk

Crumstone

Boat Trips
Sailaround
A complete tour around all the Farne Islands without landing, though with a running commentary by the boatman, including history and bird identification. These

trips allow close-up views of breeding seabird colonies and the grey seal colony. Trips run close to the red-and-white Longstone Lighthouse.

Staple Island

Generally visited in the morning, with access up a flight of stone steps onto the island. Walkways allow close-up views of bird colonies. The former lighthouse ceased service in 1784 and was replaced by one on nearby Brownsman's Island. The associated buildings are now inhabited by National Trust staff. There is a landing fee, waived for National Trust members.

Inner Farne

Generally visited in the afternoon. Walkways allow close-up views of bird colonies. There is a landing fee, waived for National Trust members. The formidable Prior Castell's Tower was built around 1500 for monastic use, then as a fort and lighthouse. A chapel dating from 1370 stands on the site of an oratory founded by St Cuthbert. The white-painted Farne Lighthouse, dating from 1801, is perched on a cliff on the far side of the island.

Longstone

The Longstone and its 20m (66ft) tall red-and-white lighthouse can be visited, and while there is no landing fee, there is an entry charge for the lighthouse. This was Grace Darling's home in September 1838 when, with her father William, she rescued survivors from the *Forfarshire*, which was wrecked on nearby Big Harcar. You can look out of Grace's bedroom window towards the rocks and try to imagine conditions during a storm.

ST CUTHBERT

Cuthbert was a Borders man through and through, born in 635AD, the year Aidan came to Lindisfarne. One night in 651AD, Cuthbert had a vision of a soul being taken up to heaven, which occurred at the moment Aidan died, so Cuthbert decided to become a monk. He travelled extensively and is associated with the monasteries at Lindisfarne, Melrose and Ripon. He lived as a hermit on Inner Farne from 676AD to 684AD, and appeared to display a special affinity with animals, in a sense becoming the first wildlife warden on the islands. He was appointed Bishop of Lindisfarne, and held the post for two years, but yearned to return to the simple life of a hermit, and spent the last two months of his life on Inner Farne, where he died in 687AD.

Cuthbert was buried at Lindisfarne, but his body was not finished travelling. After 188 years in the grave, in response to repeated Danish raids, Cuthbert's body was exhumed and carried from place to place around the Borders. According to local tradition, a church was founded at every place where the body found temporary rest. After being buried for another 113 years at Chester-le-Street, Cuthbert's body was again exhumed and carried from place to place, until finally being laid to rest in 995AD. First the 'White Church', then Durham Cathedral, was raised over his grave.

APPENDIX 1
Route summary table

Day 1	Corbridge to Allendale Town	27.5km (17 miles)
Day 2	Allendale Town to Bardon Mill	17.5km (11 miles)
Day 3	Bardon Mill to Wark	21km (13 miles)
Day 4	Wark to Elsdon	29km (18 miles)
Day 5	Elsdon to Rothbury via the Moors *Alternative Elsdon to Rothbury via the Forests*	22km (13½ miles) *21km (13 miles)*
Day 6	Rothbury to Uswayford	32km (20 miles)
Day 7	Uswayford to Wooler via the Cheviot *Alternative: Uswayford to Wooler via Linhope*	24km (15 miles) *29km (18 miles)*
Day 8	Wooler to Bamburgh via Belford *Alternative: Wooler to Bamburgh via Chillingham*	29km (18 miles) *31km (19 miles)*
Day 9	Bamburgh to Alnmouth	31km (19 miles)
	Total distance (main route)	**254km (157½ miles)**

APPENDIX 2
Accommodation list

Accommodation around the Reivers Way is unevenly spread, and there are long gaps with very little or nothing at all. In a couple of remote places there is only a single address available. Bear in mind that accommodation lists change very rapidly, with addresses coming and going all the time. The following list is very basic, and serves mainly to highlight those places with abundant, or little, accommodation. Addresses can be checked against the *Northumberland Holiday and Short Breaks Guide,* which can be obtained free of charge from tourist information centres, tel 01670 794520, www.visitnorthumberland.com.

Corbridge
Angel Inn, tel 01434 632119
Riggsacre, tel 01434 632617
Priorfield, tel 01434 633179
Town Barns, tel 01434 633345
Riverside, tel 01434 632942
Norgate, tel 01434 633736
Fellcroft, tel 01434 632384
The Hayes, tel 01434 632010

Dilston (off-route)
Dilston West Cottage, tel 01434 632464
Dilston Mill, tel 01434 633493

Devil's Water (off-route)
Travellers Rest, Slaley, tel 01434 673231
Peth Head Cottage, Low Juniper, tel 01434 673286
Dukesfield Hall Farm, tel 01434 673634

Allendale Town
King's Head, tel 01434 683681
Allendale Tea Rooms, tel 01434 683575
Hare and Hounds, tel 01434 683300

Thornley Gate
Thornley House, tel 01434 683255
Oakey Dean, tel 01434 683572

Allendale
Struthers Farm, tel 01434 683580
Staward Station, tel 01434 683030

Bardon Mill
Montcoffer, tel 01434 344138
Bowes Hotel, tel 01434 344237
Strand Cottage, tel 01434-344643

Vindolanda (off-route)
Maple Lodge, tel 01434 344365

Hadrian's Wall (off-route)
Beggar Bog, tel 01434 344652
Moss Kennels, tel 01434 344016
The Old Repeater Station, tel 01434 688668

Wark
Battlesteads Hotel, tel 01434 230209
Black Bull Inn, tel 01434 230239

Cornhills (off-route)
Cornhills Farmhouse, tel 01830 540232

Elsdon
Bird in Bush, tel 01830 520804
Old School House, tel 01830 520389
Townfoot, tel 01830 520548

Otterburn (off-route)
Butterchurn Guest House, tel 01830 520585
Percy Arms Hotel, tel 01830 520261
Otterburn Tower Hotel, tel 01830 520620
Otterburn Hall Hotel, tel 01830 520663

Rothbury
Silverton House, tel 01669 621395
The Orchard, tel 01669 620684
Queens Head Hotel, tel 01669 620470
Springfield, tel 01669 621277
The Haven, tel 01669 620577
Katerina's, tel 01669 620691
Turk's Head, tel 01669 620434

Thropton
Three Wheat Heads Inn, tel 01669 620262
Rockwood House, tel 01669 620989
Farm Cottage Guest House, tel 01669 620831
Thropton Demesne Farmhouse, tel 01669 620196

Harbottle
The Byre, tel 01669 650476

Alwinton
Coquetdale, tel 01669 650253
Rose & Thistle Inn, tel 01669 650226
Clennel Hall Hotel, tel 01669 650377

Uswayford
Uswayford Farm, tel 01669 650237

Barrowburn (off-route)
Barrowburn Camping Barn, tel 01669 621176

Wooler
Tankerville Arms Hotel, tel 01668 281581
Ryecroft Hotel, tel 01668 281459
Black Bull Hotel, tel 01668 281309
Wheatsheaf Hotel, tel 01668 281434
The Anchor Inn, tel 01668 281412
Winton House, tel 01668 281362
Cheviot View, tel 01668 281612
Rockcliffe House, tel 01668 283992
Tilldale House, tel 01668 281450
Belmont House, tel 01668 283769
Tillside, tel 01668 281252

Hazelrigg
South Hazelrigg Farmhouse, tel 01668 215216

Chatton
Percy Arms Hotel, tel 01668 215244
The Old Manse, tel 0168 215507

Belford
Blue Bell Hotel, tel 01668 213543
Farmhouse Guest House, tel 01668 213083

Market Cross Guest House, tel 01668 213013
Seafields, tel 01668 213502
Bluebell Farm Bunkbarn, tel 01668 213362

Waren Mill
Waren House Hotel, tel 01668 214581

Bamburgh
Victoria Hotel, tel 01668 214431
Lord Crewe Hotel, tel 01668 214243
The Sunningdale, tel 01668 214334
Glenander, tel 01668 214336
The Greenhouse, tel 01668 214513

Seahouses
Bamburgh Castle Hotel, tel 01665 720283
St Aidan Hotel, tel 01665 720335
Beach House Hotel, tel 01665 720337
The Olde Ship Hotel, tel 01665 720200
The Lodge, tel 01665 720158
The Old Manse, tel 01665 720521
Springwood, tel 01665 720320
Spindrift, tel 01665 721667
Sharrow, tel 01665 721794
Rowena, tel 01665 721309
Holly Trees, tel 01665 721942
Fairfield, tel 01665 721736
Mainston House, tel 01665 722922
Kingsway, tel 01665 720621
Horncliffe Guest House, tel 01665 721706
Leeholme, tel 01665 720230
Ne Oublie House, tel 01665 720108

North Sunderland
Slate Hall, tel 01665 721172
St Cuthbert's House, tel 01665 720456
Railston House, tel 01665 720912
The Olde School House, tel 01665 720760

Beadnell
New Beadnell Towers Hotel, tel 01665 721211
Beach Court, tel 01665 720225

Shepherds Cottage, tel 01665 720497
The Hemmel, tel 01665 721796

Beadnell Harbour
Shearwater, tel 01665 720654
Low Dover, tel 01665 720291
Waters Edge, tel 01665 720335

Embleton (off-route)
Dunstanburgh Castle Hotel, tel 01665 576111
Blue Bell Inn, tel 01665 576573

Boulmer
Boulmer Village, tel 01665 577262

Craster
Harbour Lights, tel 01665 576062

Dunstan (off-route)
Stonecroft, tel 01665 576433

Howick
Howick Scar Farmhouse, tel 01665 576665

Alnmouth
Schooner Hotel, tel 01665 830216
Saddle Hotel, tel 01665 830476
Beech Lodge, tel 01665 830709
Seafield House, tel 01665 833256
Sefton House, tel 01665 833174
Westlea, tel 01665 830730

Alnwick Station
Bilton Barns Farmhouse, tel 01665 830427

APPENDIX 3
Useful information

Northumberland County Council has a responsibility for the upkeep of rights of way and provides a wealth of services and facilities around the Reivers Way.

Northumberland County Council, County Hall, Morpeth, Northumberland, NE61 2EF, tel 01670 533000, www.northumberland.gov.uk

Northumberland Coast AONB, based at County Hall, Morpeth, tel 01670 534088, www.northumberlandcoastaonb.org

Northumberland National Park Authority, Eastburn, South Park, Hexham, Northumberland, NE46 1BS, tel 01434 605555, www.northumberland-national-park.org.uk

Northumberland Holiday and Short Breaks Guide, for accommodation details, tel 01670 794520, www.visitnorthumberland.com

Tourist Information Centres
Corbridge, tel 01434 632815
Hexham, tel 01434 652220
Otterburn, tel 01830 520225
Rothbury, tel 01669 620887
Wooler, tel 01668 282123
Seahouses, tel 01665 720884
Craster, tel 01665 576007
Alnwick, tel 01665 511333

Public Transport
Newcastle Airport, tel 0871 8821121, www.newcastleairport.com
DFDS Seaways, tel 0871 5229955, www.dfdsseaways.co.uk
Cross Country trains, tel 0844 811 0124, www.crosscountrytrains.co.uk
National Express East Coast, www.nationalexpresseastcoast.com
Northern Rail, www.northernrail.org
National Express coaches, tel 0871 7818181, www.nationalexpress.com
Arriva buses, tel 0870 1201088, www.arrivabus.co.uk
Snaith's buses, Otterburn, tel 01830 520609, www.howardsnaith.co.uk

Glen Valley buses, Wooler, tel 01668 281578
Travelsure buses, Belford, tel 01665 720955, www.travelsure.co.uk
Traveline North East, tel 0871 2002233, www.travelinenortheast.info

Farne Islands Ferries
Billy Shiels tel 01665 720308, www.farne-islands.com
Hanvey's tel 01665 720388, www.farneislands.co.uk
Sovereign tel 01665 720059, www.sovereigndiving.co.uk
Golden Gate tel 01665 721210, www.farneislandsboattrips.co.uk

APPENDIX 4
The Archbishop's Curse

At the peak period of reiving activity, in 1525, the Archbishop of Glasgow pronounced the following exceedingly lengthy, and remarkably comprehensive, blood-curdling curse on Scottish reiver families.

Gude folks, heir at my Archibischop of Glasgwis letters under his round sele, direct to me or any uther chapellane, makand mensioun, with greit regrait, how hevy he beris the pietous,

Depiction of St Cuthbert in a local stained glass window

S. Cuthbertus.

lamentabill, and dolorous complaint that pass our all realme and commis to his eris, be oppin voce and fame, how our souverane lordis trew liegis, men, wiffis and barnys, bocht and redeimit be the precious blude of our Salviour Jhesu Crist, and levand in his lawis, are saikleslie part murdrist, part slayne, brynt, heryit, spulziet and reft, oppinly on day licht and under silens of the nicht, and thair takis and landis laid waist, and thair self banyst therfra, als wele kirklandis as utheris, be commoun tratouris, ravaris, theiffis, dulleand in the south part of this realme, sic as Tevidale, Esdale, Liddisdale, Ewisdale, Nedisdale, and Annandereaill; quhilis hes bene diverse ways persewit and punist be the temperale swerd and our Soverane Lordis auctorite, and dredis nocht the samyn.

And thairfoir my said Lord Archbischop of Glasgw hes thocht expedient to strike thame with the terribill swerd of halykirk, quhilk thai may nocht lang endur and resist; and has chargeit me, or any uther chapellane, to denounce, declair and proclame thaim oppinly and generalie cursit, at this market-croce, and all utheris public places.

Hairfor throw the auctorite of Almichty God, the Fader of hevin, his Son, our Saviour, Jhesu Crist, and of the Halygaist; throw the auctorite of the Blissit Virgin Sanct Mary, Sanct Michael, Sanct Gabriell, and all the angellis; Sanct John the Baptist, and all the haly patriarkis and prophets; Sanct Peter, Sanct Paull, Sanct Andro, and all haly appostillis; Sanct Stephin, Sanct Laurence, and all haly mertheris; Sanct Gile, Sanct Martyn, and all haly confessouris; Sanct Anne, Sanct Katherin, and all haly virginis and matronis; and of all the sanctis and haly company of hevin; be the auctorite of our Haly Fader the Paip and his cardinalis, aned of my said Lord Archibischop of Glasgw, be the avise and assistance of my lordis, archibischop, bischopis, abbotis, priouris, and utheris prelatis and minesteris of halykirk.

I denounce, proclamis, and declaris all and sindry the committaris of the said saikles murthris, slauchteris, brinying, heirchippes, reiffis, thiftis and spulezeis, oppinly apon day licht and under silence of nicht, alswele within temporale landis as kirklandis; togither with thair partakeris, assitaris, supplearis, wittandlie resettaris of thair personis, the gudes reft and stollen be thaim, art or part thereof, and their counsalouris and defendouris, of thair evil dedis generalie CURSIT, waryit, aggregeite, and reaggregeite, with the GREIT CURSING.

I curse their heid and all the haris of thair heid; I curse thair face, thair ene, thair mouth, thair neise, thair tongue, thair teeth, thair crag, thair shoulderis, thair breist, thair hert, thair stomok, thair bak, thair wame, thair armes, thais leggis, thair handis, thair feit, and everilk part of thair body, frae the top of their heid to the soill of thair feet, befoir and behind, within and without.

I curse thaim gangand, and I curse them rydland; I curse thaim standand, and I curse thaim sittand; I curse thaim etand, I curse thaim drinkand; I curse thaim walkand, I curse thaim sleepand; I curse thaim risand, I curse thaim lyand; I curse thaim at hame, I curse thaim fra hame; I curse thaim within the house, I curse thaim without the house; I curse thair wiffis, thair barnis, and thair servandis participand with thaim in their deides. I way thair cornys, thair catales, thair woll, thair scheip, thjair horse, thair swyne, thair geise, thair hennes, and all thair quyk gude. I wary their hallis, thair chalmeris, thair kechingis, thair stanillis, thair barnys, thair biris, thair bernyardis, thair cailyardis thair plewis, thair harrowis, and the gudis and housis that is necessair for their sustentatioun and weilfair.

All the malesouns and waresouns that ever gat warldlie creatur sen the begynnyng of the world to this hour mot licht on thaim. The maledictioun of God, that lichtit apon Lucifer and all his fallowis, that strak thaim frae the hie hevin to the deip hell, mot licht apon thaimr.

The fire and the swerd that stoppit Adam far the yettis of Paradise, mot stop thaim frae the gloire of Hevin. quhill thai forbere and mak amendis. The malesound that lichtit on cursit Cayein, quhen his slew his bruther just Abell saiklessly, mot licth on thaim for the saikles slauchter that thai commit dailie. The maledictioun that lichtit apon all the warlde, man and beist, and all that ever tuk life, quhen all was drownit be the flude of Noye, except Noye and his ark, mot licht apon thame and drouned thame, man and beist, and mak this realm cummirless of thame for thair wicked synnys. The thunnour and fireflauchtis that set doun as rane apon the cities of Zodoma and Gomora, with all the landis about, and brynt thame for thair vile sunnys, mot rane apon thame, and birne thaim for oppin synnis. Tha malesoun and confusion that lichtit on the Gigantis for thair oppressioun and pride, biggand the tour of Ballloun, mot confound thaim and all thair werkis, for thair opppin reiffs and oppressioun. All the plagis that fell apon Pharao and his pepill of Egipt, thair landis, cornse, and cataill, mot fall apon thaim, thair takkis, rowmys and stedingis, cornys and beistis. The watter of Tweid and utheris watteris quhair thair ride mot droun thaim, as the Reid Say drownit King Pharoao and his pepil of Egipt, sersewing Godis pepill of Israell. The erd mot oppin, riffe and cleiff , and swelly thaim quyk to

hell, as it swellyt cursit Dathan and Abiron, that genestude Moeses and the command of God. The wyld fyre that byrnt Thore and his fallowis to the nowmer of twa hundredth and fyty, and utheris 14000 and 7000 at anys, usurpand aganis Moyses and Aaron, servandis of God, not suddanely birne and consume thaim dailie genestandand the commandis of God and halykirk. The malediction that lichtit suddanely upon fair Absalon, rydant contrair his fader, King David, servand of God, throw the wod, quhen the branchis of ane tre fred him of his horse and hangit him be the hair, mot lie apon thaain trew Scottis men, and hang thaim siclike tha all the warld may se. The Maledictioun that lichtit apon Olifernus, lieutenant to Nabogodonooser, makand weair and heirchippis apon trew cristin men, the maledictioun that lichtit apon Judas, Pylot, Herod and the Jowis that chucifyit Our Lord, and all the plagis and trublis that lichtit on the citte of Jherusalme thairfor, and upon Simon Magus for his symony, bludy Nero, cusit Ditius Makcensisu, Olibruis, Julianus Apostita and the laiff of the cruell tirrannis that slew and murthirit Crits haly servandis, mot licth apon thame for thair cruel tiranny and murthirdome of cristin pepill.

And all the vengeance that evir was takin sen the warlde began for oppin synnys, and all the plagis and pestilence that ever fell on man or beist, mot fall on thaim for thair oppin reiff, saiklesse slauchter and schedding of innocent blude. I disserver and pairtis thaim fra the kirk of God, and deliveris thaim quyk to the devill of hell, as the Apostill Sanct Paull deliverit Corinthion. I interdite the places thay cum in fra divine service, minitracioun of the sacramentis of halykirk, except the sacrament of baptissing allenerlie; and forbiddis all kirkmen to schriffe or absolbe thim of theire synnys, quhill they be firs abolyeit of this cursing.

I forbid all cristin man or woman till have ony company with thaime, etand, drynkand, spekand, prayand, lyand, gangand, standand, or in any uther deid doand, under the paine of deidly syn. I discharge all bandis, actis, contractis, athis and obligatiounis made to them by ony persounis, outher of lawte, kyndenes or manrent, salang as thai susteined this cursing, sub that na man be bundin to thaim, and that this be bundin till all men. I tak fra thame and cryis douned all the gude dedis that ever thai did or sall do, quhill thai rise froae this cursing. I declare thaim partles of of all matynys, messis, evinsangis, dirigeis or utheris prayeris, on buke or beid; of all pilgrimagis and almouse deids done or to be done in halykirk or be cristin pepill, enduring this cursing.

And, finally, I condemn thaim perpetualie to the deip pit of hell, the remain with Lucifer and all his fallowis, and thair bodeis to the gallows

Holystone (Day 6)

of the Burrow Mure, first to be hangit, syne revin and ruggit with doggis, swyne, and utheris wyld beists, abhominable to all the warld. And their candillis gangis frae your sicht, ast mot their saulis gang fra the visage of God, and thair gude faim fra the warld, quhill thai forbeir thair oppin synnys foirsaidis and ryse frae this terribill cursing, and mak satisfaction and pennance.

LISTING OF CICERONE GUIDES

For full and up-to-date information
on our ever-expanding list of guides,
please visit our website:
www.cicerone.co.uk.

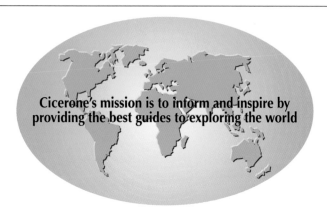

Cicerone's mission is to inform and inspire by providing the best guides to exploring the world

Since its foundation 40 years ago, Cicerone has specialised in publishing guidebooks and has built a reputation for quality and reliability. It now publishes nearly 300 guides to the major destinations for outdoor enthusiasts, including Europe, UK and the rest of the world.

Written by leading and committed specialists, Cicerone guides are recognised as the most authoritative. They are full of information, maps and illustrations so that the user can plan and complete a successful and safe trip or expedition – be it a long face climb, a walk over Lakeland fells, an alpine cycling tour, a Himalayan trek or a ramble in the countryside.

With a thorough introduction to assist planning, clear diagrams, maps and colour photographs to illustrate the terrain and route, and accurate and detailed text, Cicerone guides are designed for ease of use and access to the information.

If the facts on the ground change, or there is any aspect of a guide that you think we can improve, we are always delighted to hear from you.

Cicerone Press
2 Police Square Milnthorpe Cumbria LA7 7PY
Tel: 015395 62069 Fax: 015395 63417
info@cicerone.co.uk www.cicerone.co.uk

CICERONE